on track ...

Ian Hunter

every album, every song

G. Mick Smith

sonicbondpublishing.com

Sonicbond Publishing Limited
www.sonicbondpublishing.co.uk
Email: info@sonicbondpublishing.co.uk

First Published in the United Kingdom 2024
First Published in the United States 2024

British Library Cataloguing in Publication Data:
A Catalogue record for this book is available from the British Library

Typeset in ITC Garamond Std & ITC Avant Garde Gothic
Printed and bound in England

Graphic design and typesetting: Full Moon Media

Follow us on social media:
Twitter: https://twitter.com/SonicbondP
Instagram: www.instagram.com/sonicbondpublishing_/
Facebook: www.facebook.com/SonicbondPublishing/

Linktree QR code:

Dedications

This book is dedicated to Michael Riah who from the first time I heard him sing his song 'Whose My Friend', I knew what he was here for:

As iron sharpens iron, so a friend sharpens a friend.
Proverbs 27:17 New Living Translation

on track ...
Ian Hunter

Contents

Introduction 7

Ian Hunter...9

All American Alien Boy 15

Overnight Angels 23

You're Never Alone With A Schizophrenic.................................... 29

Welcome To The Club.. 37

Short Back 'N' Sides... 45

All Of The Good Ones Are Taken 52

Hunter's 80s Hiatus.. 57

YUI Orta.. 60

The Hunter Ronson Band BBC Live In Concert 67

Ian Hunter's Dirty Laundry... 69

The Artful Dodger.. /4

Rant 81

Strings Attached 89

The Truth, The Whole Truth And Nuthin' But The Truth 93

Shrunken Heads.. 94

Man Overboard 102

When I'm President 108

Ian Hunter And The Rant Band: Live In The UK 2010.............. 116

Fingers Crossed... 118

Stranded In Reality Box Set.. 125

Bibliography 140

Introduction

In the realm of rock 'n' roll, where legends are born and icons take the stage, there exists a rare breed of musician who defies conventions and leaves an indelible mark on fans worldwide. And in the midst of this electrifying tapestry of musical brilliance stands a figure whose name reverberates through and beyond classic rock: Ian Hunter.

In the vibrant tapestry of rock 'n' roll history, Hunter emerges as a dynamic figure, embodying the essence of rock 'n' roll from his earliest musical efforts in the 1950s to 1969, just before he embarked on a legendary journey with Mott The Hoople. With a spark of rebellious spirit and an insatiable hunger for sonic exploration, Hunter, armed with only a guitar, a vision, and a voice that could shake listeners, he honed his craft, capturing the raw energy of the era while seeking his own unmistakable style. His early years were a whirlwind of gigs in smoky clubs, crafting his songwriting, and playing in semi-pro settings. Hunter crackled with the electricity of possibility. As the clock ticked closer to 1969, a new chapter was about to unfold, setting the stage for Hunter's monumental collaboration with Mott The Hoople and solidifying his status.

Enter the realm of rock majesty, where, over time, Ian Hunter emerged as the vibrant force behind the legendary Mott The Hoople. From the moment he joined forces with the band, he unleashed a whirlwind of creativity and swagger, transforming their sound into a sonic spectacle that defied convention. With his charismatic stage presence and an arsenal of electrifying lyrics, Hunter became the beacon guiding Mott The Hoople towards greatness. But it was their David Bowie-penned signature anthem, 'All The Young Dudes', that catapulted them to immortal fame. Once he arrived at pop success, Hunter walked away from success because he was about to embark on the infectious magic of his own unforgettable opuses.

Imagine, if you will, a sonic alchemist with a pen in one hand and a guitar in the other, crafting timeless lyrical landscapes. Hunter, the singer-songwriter extraordinaire, has been the mastermind behind some of the most exhilarating rock ever recorded. From the gritty passion of 'Once Bitten, Twice Shy' to the personal defiance of 'This Is What I'm Here For', his music has stirred souls and married rock 'n' roll to classic rock and beyond under a common love for the power of music.

Hunter has produced a significant body of work; thus, there is quite a bit to be reviewed, as this is the first track-by-track book ever about his artistry. The series is designed to provide a contrast between solid, factual information and critical analysis. Hunter's comments are the primary sources I used, and Campbell Devine's Authorised Biography was indispensable. Unless stated elsewhere, all references to Ian Hunter's opinions of his own work are taken from Devine's biography or from his comments in *Ian Hunter Stranded In Reality* by Proper Records. The author is a lifelong fan and an academic by training. I hope to balance these two critical components into a compelling story about the man who I consider to be the best representative of classic rock and post-rock based on the fact that Ian heard the early rock and rollers; moreover, he had his fifteen minutes of fame in his first genuine rock band, then in a second part of his career he teamed up with one of the best guitarists of the classic rock era, and finally, he produced yet another vibrant period of high-quality works that extended the rock genre beyond classic rock.

My discussion of live performances accounts for Hunter's significant variations in arrangements, dynamics, and musicians as Ian has creatively rearranged his songs throughout his solo career. Listeners can enjoy the studio versions of songs and live alternatives, especially now with the *Stranded In Reality* massive box set as accompaniment. I analyse each song at its first mention in the book, but the reader can follow the evolution of Ian's songs since 1975.

Hunter broke the mould of classic rock, where musicians had numerous hits and then repetitively performed them live, as he wrote in 'All The Way From Memphis':

Yeah it's a mighty long way down rock 'n' roll
From the Liverpool docks to the Hollywood bowl

Ian has never been a nostalgia act, and hits were not his forte, but insightful lyrics and the quality of his music characterised his lifetime contribution. Hunter has achieved belated recognition considering the fact that, as the sales of rock have declined, Ian has reemerged on the charts for his last three studio releases. Ian has blossomed as the master of the post-classic rock era. Paradoxically, as classic rock has declined in sales as a genre, Hunter has gotten more popular: quality wins out.

I am striking a balance between the discussion of Hunter's music and lyrics. Although I am not bogged down in too much analysis of lyrical content, kindly note that the artist is an exceptionally well-read individual. Hunter is not an intellectual, but, is an intelligent individual who makes numerous historical, literary, and cultural allusions. The point of my discussion is to provide the reader with a greater appreciation of Hunter's music.

Here is the way to proceed. Each chapter stands alone thus, you can be entertained, educated, and jump in and out at any point of musical direction. Finally, the next step, if you have not joined already, is to find a community of Ian Hunter aficionados, if not in person, then online. Welcome!

Ian Hunter

Personnel:
Ian Hunter: vocals, rhythm guitar, piano, percussion, backing vocal
Mick Ronson: lead guitar, organ, Mellotron, mouth organ, bass guitar
Geoff Appleby: bass guitar, backing vocals
Dennis Elliott: drums, percussion
Pete Arnesen: piano, keyboards
John Gustafson: bass guitar on 'Lounge Lizard'
All songs written by Ian Hunter unless stated
Produced at AIR, London, by Ian Hunter and Mick Ronson
Release date: 28 March 1975
Running time: 40:38
Current edition: CBS
Highest chart places: UK: 21, US: 50

With the startling departure from his troubled band Mott The Hoople, Hunter and the Spider with the platinum hair, Mick Ronson, joined forces. Picture this: Ian finds himself settling into the cosy quarters of Rockland, New York, under the watchful eye of Bobby Colomby, the jazz-rock fusion drummer, while Colomby ventures out on tour. It is within these walls that Hunter's creative spirit ignites, giving birth to the compelling compositions of his first solo LP.

As Ronson takes flight back to England to assemble a new band, he plants the seeds of collaboration, suggesting the addition of Geoff Appleby on bass, a former comrade from their shared days in The Rats back in Hull. Intriguingly, Hunter's quest for the perfect rhythm leads him to the swing-infused prowess of drummer Dennis Elliott, whose jazz-rock background struck a harmonious chord with Ian's musical vision. But the ensemble wouldn't be complete without the enchanting melodies brought forth by the gifted Hans-Peter Arnesen, plucked from his student realm to join the ranks as the master of keys.

While Mott had already secured the legendary Air Studios in London for their next endeavour, Hunter and Ronson daringly opted for a different path, venturing into uncharted musical waters. The stage is set, the characters assembled, and the magic awaits as we unveil the captivating tale of Ian's first bold step into the realm of his own musical destiny.

Ian signed a solo deal with Columbia with the idea of taking some of the work he started in Mott but with his new direction in mind. The leftover Mott material included 'Colwater High', 'One Fine Day' and 'Lounge Lizard'. The latter song was re-recorded with the new band but the first two songs were not completed originally. Nine original tracks burst free. Only 'Boy' was co-written with Ronson; all other tracks were Hunter's.

Ian Hunter's self-titled debut album introduced the world to a raw, untamed talent whose music echoed with an unbridled spirit of rebellion and a burning desire to break free from the shackles of pop conformity that Mott The Hoople had become. With his distinct voice and poetic songwriting, Hunter captivated audiences and left an indelible mark with the hit 'Once Bitten Twice Shy'. But as the echoes of his debut faded into the distance, a new chapter was about to unfold – an evolution that would solidify Hunter's status as a true musical force. Enter the realm of his second album *All American Alien Boy*. The release would be an artistic tour de force – and commercial suicide.

'Once Bitten Twice Shy'

'Once Bitten Twice Shy' is one of Ian's best-known songs, which was both a single and an album track, and he summarises it briefly as 1970s Chuck Berry with a twist. It's a strong track that has just about everything going for it: beat, build, and restraint. In the latter part of the AIR sessions, it started with a Little Queenie rhythm guitar style vamp along with the unplanned but signature 'Allo' intro paralleling the 'Goodbye' that concluded Mott The Hoople's 'Saturday Gigs'. Building in intensity, then mid-way, Ronson's guitar sparkled, culminating in a fifteen-second vibrato held over the bridge until driven home to the final choruses. Mick doubled on bass as well.

It took Hunter ten hours to write the music and lyrics while at Mick's home when Ronson's wife Suzi brought in coffee for the effort while working at their flat behind the Albert Hall. The verse and the bridge came first using a little drum machine, but the hook took longer. One night, Ian sat with a drummer in the Speakeasy, talking about the song when the drummer made a comment and something clicked in Ian's head; this was ironic timing since they were both sitting there drunk. In any case, a bell went off for Hunter and he rushed home to write the song while saying a bit about a girl, the Mott breakup, and rock business all at once.

Hunter thinks of it as a first-rate track. The regal presence of Marc Bolan popped into the studio where Hunter and Ronson were recording and reacted by saying he always underestimated Ian: better late than never. It would be the only time they spoke.

It was a 1975 UK Top Ten hit, and Hunter was sure that it would be. Later, Guns 'n' Roses would share a manager with Great White and both wanted to record the song. Great White only sold two million copies, while Guns and Roses sold seven million on the album that it would have been featured on; that meant Hunter lost a few bob there. Oddly, the lead singer was nominated for a Grammy and the band's version was an American Top Five single in 1989. The song was later covered also by Shaun Cassidy and Status Quo.

'Who Do You Love'

'Who Do You Love' is an infectious toe-tapper with funky Sixties-style harmonica and boogie piano. British audiences favoured CBS's second single from the LP. This is a 'hey, it's a me or him babe' type of song. Hunter is asking for a decision. The lyrics mention Detroit, so some speculated that it was about a DJ there, but Ian has stated that this is not the case. He can't remember who it was written about. He enjoyed the groove. Hunter considers it a fabricated song with elements of truth. It appealed to a wide range of artists, considering that the Pointer Sisters, Def Leppard, and Joe Elliott's Down 'n' Outs recorded versions.

'Lounge Lizard'

'Lounge Lizard', although released on the first solo LP, had a bit of history. The song was originally a mechanical Mott The Hoople track as the B-side of 'Saturday Gigs'. Ronson re-did it with Roxy Music's Johnny Gustafson on bass. The re-do produced a stronger version than the original. The track features a 'Honky Tonk Women' cowbell, Ronson's guitar motif, and Gustafson's impressive bass line.

The year before Hunter met his future wife, Trudi, he was pulling women out of the Speakeasy in the middle of the night, which is the theme of the song.

The lounge lizard is what most fans imagine the rock 'n' roll lifestyle is all about, with groupies clamouring for musicians. Hunter wrote it using a girl, but as a cover-up for something else he was trying to express; maybe it is the tawdry rock life, but a fan often sees the lifestyle as glamorous. Ian confirms that the song is fictional.

'Boy' (Hunter/Ronson)

Ronno (Mick Ronson) convinced Ian to write the nine-minute atmospheric 'Boy' after leaving Mott The Hoople, and Ian wrote 'Did You See Them Run?' coupled with a poem he wrote in 1973, 'Shade's Off'. Once developed, 'Boy' became an original song. This was one of the songs that was unusual for Hunter in that it was written in the studio. It is likely the first song that Ronno and Ian worked on together and although Mick did not write the lyrics, he was instrumental in putting the band together and writing arrangements; thus, Ian felt he deserved co-writing credit.

Since Ronno did get co-songwriting credit on this, it fuelled the speculation that the lyrics refer to David Bowie and coke was certainly involved during *Diamond Dogs*. However, Ian has stated that it was a compendium of people and not about one person, specifically, Bowie, since Ian would not give away eight minutes to him. Hunter also said there is a bit of himself in the song and, if not Bowie, his manager was a target. If one person was singled out, it would be Joe Cocker, who was down on his luck in his career and Ian knew him a bit from his days at Island Records. Clearly, the song is about the toll that the rock star life can take on a person.

In the lyrical reference, life has good things to enjoy, such as *Beau Geste,* which is an adventure novel by British writer P.C. Wren from 1924, which details the adventures of three English brothers joining the French Foreign Legion.

'3,000 Miles From Here'
'3,000 Miles From Here' was released as both an album track and a B-side. The stark, ominous riff and Hunter's vocals were fantastic, but Ronson's inspirational guitar adds a great deal to the track. The simplicity of the track is effective as with an unfinished demo to highlight Ronson.

It appears to be about a groupie as Hunter conveys the sadness, guilt, and emotion of spending the night with a woman: 'And the sun will rise tomorrow/And wash my sins away/For I know that I've abused you/But I only had a day'. It was a holdover from Mott and Ian has said it was a sad song but realistically about how it was in the early days; the groupies can be both sad and romantic. It was partly written already but finished in the studio at the last minute because they were one song short for the solo LP.

'The Truth, The Whole Truth, Nuthin' But The Truth'
The slow, funky burn of 'The Truth, The Whole Truth, Nuthin' But The Truth' is captivating and love gone wrong is a perennial topic of interest in pop songs. It's a great combination of Hunter's vocal, Ronson's guitar, and the driving backbeat that makes this song so strong. It is one of those honest love songs similar to 'Bastard'. Ian says the lyrics are ambiguous, but he wrote it musically with Mick's guitar in mind for his incredible playing, in particular, the middle scream section. Ronno dove right in and the slow, simplicity of the song lets the guitar soar. Just before the AIR Studios session, Mick saw a review for his unappreciated *Play Don't Worry* LP that was vicious and personal. Ronson read the review, internally charged, and burnt his searing solo in response. Take that! Mick laid it down in five minutes.

'It Ain't Easy When You Fall'
With 'It Ain't Easy When You Fall', Hunter is saying that fame and success are fleeting, employing tender verses, intelligent piano interludes and captivating harmony-laden choruses. This song is unusual in that the song segues into the spoken-word poem 'Shades Off'. The subject matter is Mick Ralphs, who Ian relates really did talk about ships and boats as topics related in the song rather than getting down to the needed musical business. This is Ian's sendoff to Ralphs, who was off to Bad Company, but he still considers him a friend. It appears that Hunter is suggesting that Mick was down and out, but life moves faster. Ian and Ralpher did write solid rock while together and there is a sense of genuine loss in the song. Ian is suggesting that Mick has more to offer and has to pick himself up. Maybe Bad Company was the result.

'Shades Off'
The spoken word poem 'Shades Off' is the coda to 'It Ain't Easy When You Fall'. It was written as a poem on a short tour of Scotland with Mott The Hoople in early 1973. Ian sent off the words to be published, but it never made it into print; however, Hunter was inspired by the countryside as he

is half Scot and in the tour bus, he looked out the window and the words just started coming. The entire poem took maybe ten minutes. Poems had already appeared on *Mott* with a D.H. Lawrence contribution and Baudelaire on *Mad Shadows*. The poem was included when the album was running short of material. It served the purpose of getting a poem published and it helped the sequencing of the album. It is clearly a self-conscious personal poem of Hunter's. The 'uncontrollable light' phrase in the poem is when songwriting emerges perfectly; Ian has felt that maybe half a dozen times in his career.

'I Get So Excited'

This rocker closes out the first LP and it is a straight-ahead barn burner. The impressive debut album closes out with vibrant verses, a simple chorus, and gleeful lyrics; it starts and keeps up a frenetic pace about the buzz and fandom of music. The sequencing of the album is perfectly ended with this ode to the power and passion of rock music. There was discussion for the track as a single release, which seems reasonable since it features a stirring and driven Mick Ronson solo and Dennis Elliot's powerful drumming. CBS thought the track was more commercial and favoured its release, but Hunter liked it the least and it almost didn't get released at all. There were numerous outtakes and needing a track among others, this one was fished out by Ronson from other songs to finish in a rush. As a result, Hunter's voice wasn't all that strong, so they added every echo in the book.

The excitement has to do with music and crowds, as at Wembley or parades. Even if it's the end, he says, 'I don't care', and it could even be tied back to music since he's a fan. The song speeds up to end the LP on a high, fast note.

Related Songs

'Colwater High' has been around for a considerable amount of time. Originally, it was conceived as a possible follow-up to Mott The Hoople's 'Foxy Foxy' in 1974. Then, this song was resurrected for the first Hunter LP, but it did not see the light of day. Ian had no lyrics for the music. He didn't write the lyrics until 30 years later, but oddly enough, these words and lyrics for 'One Fine Day' came in about half an hour.

It seems as though the lyrics are describing a love but termed 'High' and he counts out 1-4, so maybe he means a high school. It is not clear, although the lyrics are among the most intricate he has written. Since he is a slave always, perhaps he means the memories and importance of troubled youthful years.

'One Fine Day' was first conceived in Mott, but it is an outtake from the first Ian Hunter LP and Ian hated it with a passion, but drummer Dennis Eliot thought it was so good it should have been a hit once Ian had recorded new vocals.

The 30th-anniversary bonus tracks include: 'Colwater High' (3:12), 'One Fine Day' (2:21), 'Once Bitten Twice Shy' (single version) (3:52), 'Who Do

You Love' (single version) (3:17), 'Shades Off' (poem) (1:37), 'Boy' (single version) (6:25)

The first Ian Hunter solo effort made a splash, but his second release proved to be more difficult.

All American Alien Boy

Personnel

Ian Hunter: lead vocals, rhythm guitar, piano on 'All American Alien Boy',
backing vocals

Chris Stainton: piano, organ, Mellotron, bass guitar on 'Restless Youth'

Jaco Pastorius: bass guitar on all tracks, guitar on track 'God (Take 1)'

Aynsley Dunbar: drums

Jerry Weems: lead guitar

David Sanborn: saxophone

Dominic Cortese: accordion

Cornell Dupree: guitar on 'Letter To Brittania From The Union Jack'

Don Alias: congas

Arnie Lawrence: clarinet

Dave Bargeron: trombone

Lewis Soloff: trumpet

Freddie Mercury: backing vocals on 'You Nearly Did Me In'

Brian May: backing vocals on 'You Nearly Did Me In'

Roger Taylor: backing vocals on 'You Nearly Did Me In'

Bob Segarini: backing vocals

Ann E. Sutton: backing vocals

Gail Kantor: backing vocals

Erin Dickins: backing vocals

All songs by Ian Hunter unless shown

Produced at Electric Lady Studios, New York City, by Ian Hunter

Release date: 29 May 1976

Running time: 69:34

Current edition: Columbia

Highest chart places: UK: 29, US: 177

The outsider Hunter unravelled the enigmatic nature of America in his
second LP, deemed by Ian as nothing short of 'commercial suicide'. Alas,
the harmonious partnership between Hunter and the incomparable Ronson
would be derailed for a staggering three years by the relentless machinery of
the music business. The virtuoso Ronno found himself irresistibly lured by
the call of countless other artists, yearning to engage him for production or
session work. Hunter was years ahead of commercial pop until the third part
of his career, when the promise of this LP emerged full-blown with his later
stellar efforts.

The legendary Bob Dylan invited Mick to tour after the pair met Dylan
when they went to New York's Bleecker Street to see Bob Neuwirth play
a spontaneous gig at The Other End. Unlikely for Ronson, who described
Bob as 'Fuckin' Yogi Bear', he nonetheless joined the travelling menagerie
of Dylan and company in October 1975 as The Rolling Thunder Revue. Also,
strangely, Bob turned out to be a Mott The Hoople fan and knew Hunter's

work; Ronson invited Ian to show up for the rolling band, but without an official invite, he passed.

Hunter, now an American emigre, absorbed around-the-clock TV, political corruption, high energy, and the madhouse landscape of New York. The move elicited a great awakening of writing, and ideas came faster and heavier than previously for Ian. Never content with the past and boredom, the next project would be a startling first impression of America filled out with a new musical direction, thought-provoking observations, and artistic freedom. The album reminds some of Dylan, Randy Newman, and John Lennon.

The supportive Bobby Colomby assisted with forming a new band of jazz-based players married to Hunter's intelligent songwriting. The core of the band turned out to be Aynsley Dunbar, drums, saxophonist David Sunburn, guitarist Jerry Weems, and on keyboards Chris Stainton. Ian felt that he had the best and he got out of their way and allowed them freedom to contribute musically themselves. The final key component came from Colomby as well when one day Ian was introduced to the young but still relatively unknown phenomenon Jaco Pastorius on bass. Pastorius invented a distinctive bass style known as 'the Jaco growl'.

The album was recorded at the famous Electric Lady Studios in Greenwich Village, NYC starting in January 1976 for three weeks. The entire process took only twenty-six days. Several tracks were first or second takes, with all the songs written, produced, and arranged by Hunter. Four numbers did not make the cut: 'Common Disease', 'If the Slipper Don't Fit', 'Whole Lotta Shakin'', and 'A Little Star'. These songs were either too fast for the rest of the completed songs on the LP or had unfinished lyrics.

The eight tracks of British American reflections, all written by Hunter, were sprinkled with jazz artistry, generally gentle songs, and poetic elements which delighted many music critics, including yours truly as a young man yearning for meaning, but the effort startled Hunter fans. Ever the innovator, Ian ignored commercial expectations, but the generally conceptual record was filled with intelligent wordplay, original arrangements, and observations about Britain, America, young love, the Mafia, rape, drugs, corporate decline, political corruption, rock 'n' roll, and God, all on one rock LP! The LP was arresting at the time but the promise of it anticipates much of Hunter's later intelligent works indicative of ideas he revisited in the remainder of his career.

'Letter To Britannia From The Union Jack'
Originally entitled 'To Rule Britannia From Union Jack', the opening track of the LP addresses a concern about Great Britain that Ian raises from time to time and increasingly and profoundly throughout his career. Not surprisingly, on an album about his first impressions of America from a recent transplant, he reviews his thoughts about his homeland, England. He recognizes the slow decline of Britannia, symbolized as the helmeted female warrior holding a trident and shield from the perspective of the Union Jack flag. It is a lament

about England as 'just a victim of your history', but the glory of England remains firmly on the masted flag. The Union Jack pleads, 'do not lower me by half'. The sentiment of the song is sad, but it implies the hope that Britannia may rise again. The song was a comment on Ian's feelings about the sorry state of Seventies England; his feelings are complicated, but this is how he felt at the time.

'All American Alien Boy'

The title track started with Gerry Weems' piercing guitar, which cut in sharply on the fade out of 'Letter To Britannia From The Union Jack'. 'All American Alien Boy' had interesting origins and although Ronson was not fated to be on Hunter's LP, he had a hand in the song. Bobby Colomby invited Mick and Ian to meet Jaco Pastorius, bass player extraordinaire and the quartet's jam was captured on 'It Never Happened' with a Super 8 cine film of their initial effort.

The seven-minute tour de force was a lyrical discourse perfectly integrating jazz-laden brass, an inspired bass interlude from Jaco, blues, and a bit of funk with Weems' guitar and Sanborn's gutsy sax. Artfully sprinkled with both British and American allusions, the collage creatively addressed the trans-Atlantic cultural voyage of Hunter.

This is one of Ian's most well-known tracks, available in numerous versions. The musicians, most notably for this song, Jaco Pastorius on bass, did it Hunter's way on the album, but for the single, it was performed the musicians' way.

The lyrics of the song describe an outsider's view of America in the 1970s. Ian found America 'tacky' as his first impression as compared to Britain. He makes a reference to John Lennon since the ex-Beatle had beat a retreat to America as well. Ian takes on the commercialism of television and references the prices of hamburgers, televisions, hotdogs and pizzas. A political point Hunter makes occasionally is about guns, as he does so here with a point about Saturday Night Specials. The phrase is a colloquial term in the United States for inexpensive, compact, and small-calibre handguns. Guns pop up in Hunter's live recasting of 'Now Is the Time'. Mary Tyler Moore was one of the important television stars back then, starring in *The Mary Tyler Moore Show* (1970–1977), which helped define a new vision of American womanhood. He closed out the song by reciting a rap-like list of Native American chiefs which he relates took a long time. Ian's appreciation of Native American history is revisited in 'Ta Shunka Witco (Crazy Horse)'. Finally, one of the most striking political lines is: 'Don't want to vote for the left-wing – don't want to vote for the right – I gotta have both to make me fly'.

'Irene Wilde'

'Irene Wilde' from Ian's second LP is one of the most well-known, beloved, and most often played of all Hunter originals. The song is a classic coming-of-age song for so many of us young boys growing up. We have that first crush and then she breaks our heart. In Ian's case, this incident was the point of growing up and motivated him to confess: 'I'm gonna be somebody – someday'.

Hunter actually started his songwriting career based on this rejection and composed all his early songs for her. Thank you, Irene! As a result, we have the output that Ian has produced all from this key youthful rejection:

And I think most folks agree, a little put-down makes them see
They ain't no chain – just a link and that's why you made me think
Gonna be somebody – be somebody – be somebody – someday

Hunter was that sixteen-year-old who ran letters between Irene and a guy she went out with at Shrewsbury High School. According to Ian, she had an irresistible Julie Christie jawline; Christie was a British actress and an icon of the Swinging 1960s.

Irene really did snub Ian at the bus station, later married, had twins, and he never saw her again but heard she liked the song. The Barker Street bus station is a car park now. At first, the song was not going to be on the album since Hunter thought the melody was too much like Bach's 'Air On A G-String', but manager Fred Heller insisted the song was included on the album and of course, he was right, as Ian says: for once!

The confessional nature of Hunter's ballad on this song is similar to the emotional impact of 'Waterlow' and 'I Wish I Was Your Mother' and was immortalised as one of his finest autobiographical efforts.

'Restless Youth'

Gerry Weems offered a robust guitar part for 'Restless Youth', which is a medium-paced song that sparked up the LP with a song similar to what Ian knew from his past. Chris Stanton played bass on this one track in a style reminiscent of Joe Cocker's 'With A Little Help From My Friends'. This song, although not American and autobiographical, seems similar to Hunter's British upbringing since he, too, had a restless youth. The Little Italy son is the leader of the gang. He is part of the criminal element and becomes a hitman, but his life is ended by a policeman. Ian's observation of America addresses the juvenile delinquency that he observed as a newly transplanted emigrant. Ian notes that it probably came from a newspaper story of the time and he was labelled 'hostile' on a school report; he still has the report.

'Rape'

'Rape' is hauntingly political but with a beautiful gospel flavour and a stunning female chorus about a violent and personal encounter. Justice is not served is the message, while the perpetrator believes he will escape punishment because he's 'sick, rich, and stoned'. The final verdict is: 'Justice just is ... Not' punctuated by majestic backing vocals.

'Singin' In The Rain' by Gene Kelly was the original intro for the song and similar to the juxtaposition between high art and violence in *A Clockwork Orange*'. Kelly rang Fred Heller, Hunter's manager, and felt the inclusion of his song might tarnish his image and the intro was dropped in 1976. Upon the reissue, Kelly had passed away in the meantime and maybe Sony took advantage of his passing and released the Kelly intro, although the label denied it and said it was a mistake. In any event, the intro works and supports the point that Ian was making. Violent criminals take advantage of society and often, there is no justice for victims.

'You Nearly Did Me In'

The majestic 'You Nearly Did Me In' started off as a song entitled 'Weary Anger' but ultimately featured the members of Queen on backing vocals: Freddie Mercury, Brian May and Roger Taylor. It was all happenstance; Trudi, Ian's wife, met Queen on a flight to New York and invited them to Electric Lady studio that night. Unbelievably, they sat and waited for an hour before Hunter knew they were there waiting and wanting to help. Freddie asked: 'Is there anything we can do?'; Instead of using backing girl vocals as arranged to sing, the boys stepped in. Roger took the really high lines and increasingly sang higher. Mott The Hoople and Queen had a long history together and Ian thought the band was fabulous and wonderful. Hunter said Freddie was sorely missed. David Sanborn contributes a fabulous sax on the track.

The first verse is about the lost children of the night and then the chorus builds up to the repeated lines of you nearly did me in. The crescendo bursts with the immortal lines:

What ever happened to dignity
What ever happened to integrity
What ever happened to honesty
Well I'll tell you something baby – I feel the pain just like the sea

The song is a standout of the LP, portraying a stark American landscape amidst the horrors of addiction.

'Apathy 83'

There is an alternate version, although it is unclear if this is just another studio take or a demo and the song of unknown provenance is simply entitled 'Apathy', while the regular release of the song 'Apathy 83' emerged on the album. The number 83 has no obvious reference.

With accordion and congas, Hunter captures aspects of Dylan's work, but he makes it his own by describing the decline of rock 'n' roll to give way to the music of the young and the sickly sound of greed. There are several intriguing aspects of the lyrics in this song and as typical on the album release, Ian is making profound social observations. Most important is Ian's observation that the music business was declining drastically, replaced by coke and corporations. In several verses, he states that there is 'no rock 'n' roll, no more just the music of the youth', 'greed', and 'rich'. In 1976, the music industry was dominated by a few major record labels, such as CBS, RCA, and Warner Communications.

With the title, Hunter makes an offhand reference to 'Sympathy For The Devil' by The Rolling Stones. 'Sympathy' is a track from The Rolling Stones' 1968 album *Beggars Banquet*. Hunter confirms that the song is related to the Stones. He relates a story that he had just seen the Stones at Madison Square Garden, and who should he meet at the concert but Bob Dylan. Bob asked him what he thought of their show; Ian responded: 'Insipid' and Dylan responded 'apathy for the devil'. Dylan gave Hunter the idea for the song. The rock 'n' roll of Little Richard and Fats Domino, according to Hunter, was associated with innocence, while the 1970s apathy was only punctuated by David Bowie.

Another important theme is social upheaval in punk rock. Bands such as the Sex Pistols, The Clash (big fans of Mott The Hoople), and The Ramones gained popularity with their anti-establishment message and DIY approach to music production.

References to the American Civil War and 'gone with the wind' tie in with the themes of power and violence in the song. Rhetorically, he asks: 'Was it your General Sheridan who once said, 'The only good, good man is a dead good man'. It wasn't Sheridan because he transferred from command of an infantry division in the Western Theatre to lead the Cavalry Corps of the Army of the Potomac in the East; thus, he was not in the March to Atlanta associated with the phrase gone with the wind. Sherman's March to the Sea was a military campaign conducted through Georgia in 1864 by William Tecumseh Sherman.

Moreover, the quote 'The only good, good man is a dead good man' fits in well with ideas of power and violence and is commonly attributed to the character Deke Thornton, played by Robert Ryan, in Sam Pekinpah's 1969 film *The Wild Bunch*. Hunter must have liked the film so much that he wrote a song entitled 'The Wild Bunch'.

The phrase 'gone with the wind' refers to the well-known book and film of the same name when the tide of war turned against the Confederacy after the Battle of Gettysburg. In one of the most brutal experiences during the war, Sherman commanded a scorched earth policy against the South and the phrase 'war is hell' is usually attributed to him. As experienced by many Southerners, Scarlett, the leading character in *Gone With The Wind*, loses her beau, Rhett, to the war. With her home deserted and pillaged by Union troops and the fields untended, she finally finds out that her mom died of typhoid fever while her father lost his mind.

'God (Take 1)'

'God (Take 1)' was originally issued on *All American Alien Boy*, but there is also '(God) Advice To A Friend' (Alternate Version) and '(God) Advice To A Friend', which is a session outtake with Jaco Pastorius on bass and guitar.

This is a witty and thought-provoking dialogue between the writer and the Almighty, with God explaining good, evil, faith, superstition, and life. This was a deliberate parody of Bob Dylan as Hunter imitated him. The goal is to be considerate in life and the actual target is the money and power that often comes with religious institutions. Hunter said: 'It's one of the best things I've written'.

Lyrically, the song is about the eternal battle between good and evil within us all. There is no preaching but just questions and speculation about the forces of good and evil, the composition of the universe, and the nature of religion. Although 'God' is about a weighty subject matter, Hunter finishes the song simply and positively 'behave yourself', and in an off-hand way, God appears to respond 'see you around'. The message seems to be that it's all going to be ok.

Conclusion

The 30th Anniversary bonus tracks include: 'To Rule Britannia From Union Jack' (Session Outtake) (4:08), 'All American Alien Boy' (Early Single Version) (4:03), 'Irene Wilde (Number One)' (Session Outtake) (3:53), 'Weary Anger' (Session Outtake) (5:45), 'Apathy' (Session Outtake) (4:42), '(God) Advice To A Friend' (Session Outtake) (5:34).

The reaction to the LP was mixed at best. Hunter feels that it was quite an accomplishment to have written about both rape and God on one record fuelled by his manager's supply of Colombian Red. He proved he could hold more than his own with top-notch musicians, but really, no one came close to the brilliance of his lyrics.

In the first week of its American release, the LP sold 56,000 copies and it entered the UK at number 47 on 29 May and stayed for four weeks, rising to number 29. In America, the LP peaked at number 177 on *Billboard*. With promotion and critical acclaim, the LP would have expected to sell more. Two singles from the LP, 'All American Alien Boy' and 'You Nearly Did Me In', died in sales terms.

Ian recognised that his ranting manifesto might leave fans behind and he philosophically exclaimed that he hoped people who liked his music would come along on his musical journey. As a commercial effort, it flopped, but on a personal level, it was a total success. He consistently has refused to be boring and this record was the first indication that Hunter was always going to listen to the beat of his own drummer. Ian's fan base consisted largely of young males and it was quite a leap to think that most young guys were going to come along for the ride. It would take some time, but the record stands as an early achievement of the grand themes and intelligent lyrics that would come to fruition later in his recordings. Interesting rock does not always sell, but it confirms that Hunter is an artist first and foremost.

To go on the road to support the release, there were rehearsals with soulful, funky R&B group The Fabulous Rhinestones, but nothing came of it. Hunter had had first-rate jazz-rock session musicians and could have gone in that direction, or with mellow songs from *All American Alien Boy*; he could continue in that vein. However, Ian was neither Jeff Beck nor the Moody Blues, so neither direction appeared promising. Hunter had already recorded proto-punk with songs such as 'Violence' and 'Crash Street Kidds' and that was also a possibility. Ian had no supporting band to go on the road to promote the album, or Hunter could pick up a trendy space he had already explored in Mott The Hoople; in short, he was in a bind. In what direction should he go?

After the electrifying journey through *All American Alien Boy*, where Ian Hunter showcased his visionary artistry and poetic prowess, the stage was set for the next chapter in his musical odyssey. As the dust settled and the echoes of his second album lingered in the air, a new wave of sonic exploration beckoned. *Overnight Angels*, Ian Hunter's third LP, was yet another LP that seemed like the death knell of commercial success.

Overnight Angels

Personnel
Ian Hunter: lead and harmony vocals, rhythm guitar, piano
Earl Slick: lead, rhythm and slide guitars
Peter Oxendale: keyboards
Rob Rawlinson: bass, harmony vocals
Dennis Elliott: drums
Miller Anderson: harmony vocals
Lem Lubin: harmony vocals
Roy Thomas Baker: percussion
Produced at: Le Studio, Morin-Heights, Quebec; Utopia Studios, Primrose Hill,
London; Olympic Studios, London, Roy Thomas Baker
Release date: May 1977
Running time: 37:33
Current edition: Columbia
Highest chart places: AU: 38, Failed to chart in the UK or US

Ian Hunter was at a crossroads, torn between the delicate allure of his jazz-rock sensibilities and the rebellious fire that courses through his rocker's veins. At the same time, a tantalising conundrum emerged as he found himself offered enticing opportunities with none other than Uriah Heep and The Doors. For Uriah Heep, Hunter was tempted to do their ten-week American tour for $5,000 a week in 1976 dollars. The Easy Street of fame and fortune was swiftly dismissed, and these tempting offers were dismissed. And what of the whispers of a revitalised Mott The Hoople? Ah, but Hunter quashed those rumours with a resolute shake of his head, having spent six years with them carving out his own vision and with no desire to revisit the painful past. Ian Hunter fearlessly forged his own path.

What Hunter envisioned was an energetic rock band format as he got acquainted with the New York new wave punk rock scene. As a first foray for bandmates, Ronson had introduced Ian to Billy Cross, who was putting the Topaz group together, and they collaborated on writing 'Crazy Glue' one day at Hunter's house. The song has never been released. At the same time, Mick Jones was forming Foreigner and Ian realised that British musicians needed work, so it occurred to him that the UK was a great recruiting field.

The new band started off strong. Hunter snagged Peter Oxendale for keyboards and as musical arranger, drummer Mac Poole, and bassist Rob Rawlinson. Once back in New York, he also recruited Earl Slick on guitar with 'Golden Opportunity' and 'I Think You Made A Mess Of His Life' (later 'Shallow Crystals') and on this basis, the next effort already had a name: *Overnight Angels*. Roy Thomas Baker had clout at CBS and appeared to be the ideal producer for the band. Recording in January and February 1977 at Le Studio in Quebec, the band had state-of-the-art equipment in a glorious setting.

Yet, issues quickly arose. Mac Poole was not working out, so he was let go with a generous financial send-off; Dennis Elliott took a break from Foreigner, but he was known to be reliable from the *Ian Hunter* LP and he was called in for support. Perhaps the venture should have had a hint of doom since luggage had been lost at the airport, there were several car crashes, Elliott's drums came unhinged on the way to the studio, and then, tragically, the entire project came to an abrupt halt on the night of 3 February when the studio housing caught fire.

The album was released in America and in Great Britain in May 1977 with singles to promote and an eight-date UK tour for June. Hunter was back to perform for British audiences for the first time in two years. Tracks were written by Hunter, except for one song.

'Golden Opportunity'

The production and management issues notwithstanding, lyrically, 'Golden Opportunity' is a fine track about England. Live this curtain raiser commenced with a meandering instrumental overture with twists and turns that featured a killer riff with Slick's guitar, Oxendale's on-target staccato piano, and great bass runs by Rawlinson.

The target is subtle, but Ian is attacking not the people but the elites who run the country. Hunter actually hates the people running the country, yet the lyrics are positive. Ian's guitar got him the opportunity he was looking for; otherwise, he said he'd be in jail. In short, it's a really positive and upbeat song about taking chances as a golden opportunity. This song is, unfortunately, one of those good songs that got buried because of music business issues.

'Shallow Crystals'

'Shallow Crystals' began life as 'I Think You Made A Mess Of His Life' and was a relaxed but acidic piece. The target is not clear but it is possible that he refers to Guy Stevens, David Bowie, or Verden Allen, and is similar to off-hand references in 'Boy'.

This is an unusual take on the 'show business mom' phenomenon. The mother pushes the kid to be a star, but she doesn't really seem to care after all. She makes a mess of the child's life.

Hunter worked closely with Earl Slick to create the guitar solo at his house in Chappaqua. Often, this was his procedure with Ronno, where he worked out a solo for hours. Ian knew what he wanted, but he couldn't score or play it, so he collaborated with a guitarist to get the sound he wanted. Possibly, this is just a collection of words and ideas that clicked, but Ian likes this song more than others on the LP.

'Overnight Angels'

The anthemic and mystical title track 'Overnight Angels' could be a reference to Hunter's penchant for Native American allusions with references to the 'Indian summer', 'Appalachian Way' and spirituality. Ian does admit it was prefabricated, though he liked the sound of the words and after the last more mellow album, *All American Alien Boy,* he was striving for more of a harder, metal sound. This was his 'plastic attempt' to get it back. Unfortunately, buried in the mix, Hunter asks at one point, 'Can you hear us?' and it sounds like it is his plea against the production. The song showcases fine piano, solo voice, and an orchestral and vocal coda by long-time Hunter mate Miller Anderson. It does figure well in the soundtrack for *Asphaltnacht*, a moody, low-budget German film about a rock musician searching for songwriting inspiration.

'Broadway'

'Broadway' is a fine ballad and a moody reflection of show business traumas. Hunter showcases his piano and vocals backed by a Broadway-style choir. Perhaps reminiscing of Mott The Hoople as the first rock band on Broadway, this ditty is about a girl who is seeking success on The Great White Way.

The production limitations of the LP notwithstanding, 'Broadway' is a standout track. Hunter thinks a great deal about 'Broadway' and he considers it among the best slow songs he's ever written. The downside, according to Ian, is the lack of an effective hook and chorus. Although there are numerous rock life types of tunes in the Hunter oeuvre this song is similar except applied to aspirations of stage stardom. The words contrast the lights of Broadway with the darkness of the aspirant:

But chances are you'll find out on Broadway
Who you really are.

Brilliant.

'Justice Of The Peace'

'Justice Of The Peace' is both a single and album track that Ian thought could be a hit, but he related that it was fabricated. The track is marred by a mix that is too high for his voice; nonetheless, the song and lyrics are sound. It's a humorous song about a shotgun wedding and a call for a Justice of the Peace to marry the unlucky couple. Oxendale samples Mendelssohn's 'Wedding March' and the song had punch with power, a great pace, and a first-rate hook.

'(Miss) Silver Dime' (Hunter, Earl Slick)

'(Miss) Silver Dime' is an ode to Alice as a 'drunken Mona Lisa' and was based on a Slick guitar lick, great piano, and good melody and chorus. This Alice is closer to a Lounge Lizard than the 'Alice' from Mott The Hoople's *The Hoople* LP, but, in fact, Ian does not know anyone named Alice. 'Silver

Dime' seems to be attracted to the rock 'n' roll lifestyle and connects with the singer. Earl Slick got a co-writing credit on the tune on this song which took only about ten minutes to write. It was to be the first single from the LP and it was written naturally.

'Wild 'N' Free'
'Wild 'N' Free' drives as hard as a pile driver kicked in with a phased drum intro before a slew of guitars and bass frantically hit. This song could be autobiographical in that it describes much of Hunter's young life. He was stuck in dead-end jobs as a young person. As he broke out and went on the road his 'babe' did not understand as most people don't, and they follow what they have been told and what is on the TV. Ian could out-punk the young kids of his day but with a maturity that they could not match in literacy and verbal fury. Hunter reminisces that it was a track that came together fast.

'The Ballad Of Little Star'
'The Ballad Of Little Star' has a bit of history as it began as 'A Little Star' during the *Alien Boy* sessions. As resurrected, it was Ian also reminiscing about being on a reservation in Canada during Mott The Hoople that inspired the song. A little organ grinder circus-like intro begins the track and then smoulders with sparse piano. This is one of the topics that Ian visits occasionally about Native Americans, as with 'Ta Shunka Witco (Crazy Horse)' and 'River Of Tears', stating 'the reservation killed your nation'. As Little Star's father explained:

Bowed those fine heads that, once proud, roamed the plains
They sought nothing to gain 'til our fathers civilised
And broken hearted arrows roamed the skies
Then you were born to feel the pain
Little Star

'To Love A Woman'
Original album closer 'To Love A Woman' is the penultimate song on the remastered CD *Overnight Angels* and is a more traditional love song, unlike 'Bastard'. Hunter thought that this would be a good vehicle for Rod Stewart to sing; it never reached him, though. The key is too high for Ian and sounds more in Stewart's range. The love song contained production tricks, multilayered chorus vocals, and a style that could have been done by The Fabulous Rhinestones.

Related Song
'England Rocks'
Ian has said he had placed himself in a stupid position by 1977 and had fired his American musicians, crew, and manager. But on a British tour, CBS

Records suddenly demanded a single product. Hunter had written 'Cleveland Rocks' about a year before and in a panic, he changed 'Cleveland' to 'England'. The song is along the same lines as 'Roll Away The Stone' and 'All The Way From Memphis'. The record stiffed until Ronson got his hands on it subsequently.

'England Rocks' is an everyman type of song glorifying the impulse to rock and subsequently, it was applied appropriately to fans in the mid-level to small cities in the United States who embraced rock acts that came to their town. It is more appropriate to the States with a reference to 'American dreams' and James Dean, who is best remembered as a cultural icon of teenage disillusionment and social estrangement.

Conclusion

The good news for the LP was that Hunter recovered from his previous effort to hone his rock roots, but the bad news is that the mix was thin, and the production did not always work to his advantage. Ian takes responsibility for the result, but an overarching issue with the production is Baker's light touch, while Hunter's style leans towards a heavy approach. In retrospect, Ian thinks some of the rough mixes might have presented his songs and voice better.

Most of the UK press greeted the release warmly. Elliott returned to Foreigner, so Walter 'Curly' Smith got the nod for the live shows and he was able to add an awesome harmonica to the proceedings. From the 3rd to the 12th of June the band toured England, but once Ian fired his manager Fred Heller, the band was stuck in low gear, but dates on the Continent were added to keep the group together.

With no material and caught in a lurch, Hunter hurriedly released a song on 22 July 1977 that he had originally written as 'Cleveland Rocks' but re-done as 'England Rocks'. It was a non-LP single, but the record died. Adding to his woes, suddenly Columbia Records refused to release the LP in America.

With punk and new wave all the rave and Hunter releasing two back-to-back commercially unsuccessful albums and a dead-end single, it was time to reevaluate or anticipate the end of his career. It might have been time to consider the end seriously with no management, record company support, and a band that began to fragment with few prospects. Back in New York, Hunter played keyboards on the first Tuff Darts LP.

Was it time for the outsider to hang it up?

Witness the phoenix-like transformation as Ian Hunter evolves from the rebellious rock energy of *Overnight Angels* to the unparalleled brilliance of *You're Never Alone With A Schizophrenic*. Like a lightning bolt of musical innovation, Hunter sheds his former skin, embracing a new sonic identity that is both audacious and electrifying. With infectious hooks, relentless energy, and thought-provoking lyrics, this album is a sonic revolution. Collaborating with legendary producer and guitarist extraordinaire Ronson, Hunter unleashes a sonic tapestry that melds rock into a genre-defining masterpiece.

From the anthemic 'Cleveland Rocks' to the soul-stirring introspection of 'Ships', each track is a testament to Hunter's unparalleled artistry and an invitation to immerse yourself in his captivating world.

You're Never Alone With A Schizophrenic

Personnel

Ian Hunter: lead vocals, guitar, piano, Moog, ARP, organ, harmony vocals, percussion

Mick Ronson: guitars, dual lead vocals on 'When The Daylight Comes', harmony vocals, percussion

Roy Bittan: ARP, organ, Moog, piano, harmony vocals

Max Weinberg: drums

Garry Tallent: bass

John Cale: piano, ARP on 'Bastard'

George Young: tenor saxophone

Lew Delgatto: baritone saxophone

Ellen Foley: harmony vocals

Rory Dodd: harmony vocals

Eric Bloom: harmony vocals

Produced at: The Power Station, New York City, by Ian Hunter and Mick Ronson

Release date: 23 April 1979

Running time: 42:04

Current edition: Chrysalis

Highest chart places: UK: 49, AU: 68, US: 35

As the ink dried on his contract with Chrysalis, a harmonious blend of talent and astute management from the esteemed Cleveland International paved the way for the birth of a new band. In the humble confines of a public restroom, Ronson's keen eye caught sight of a poignant slogan scrawled upon a bog wall. Hunter loved the slogan, and to gain access to its use, he bestowed co-writing credit upon Ronson and used 'you're never alone with a schizophrenic' as the album's title. Needing exceptional musicians for the effort, Glen Matlock was tapped for bass, drummer Clive Bunker, and then, fortuitously, the core members of the E Street Band. The musicians were filled out with 'Professor' Roy Bittan on piano, Max Weinberg on drums, and Garry W. Tallent on bass.

Hunter's next steps would be to find his place as an outsider. On 23 December 1977 at Friars Aylesbury, Hunter joined former Mott The Hoople bandmates in British Lions and sang 'All The Young Dudes', which was their first musical connection since the original band had disbanded. Then, Hunter was asked to produce Mr. Big and added piano, organ, and guitar during the sessions, along with Peter Oxendale on keyboards. The result was *Seppuku*, a hard rock effort that was buried by EMI Records for over twenty years. 'Señora' was co-written by Ian but was not released at the time; this is a terrific power ballad about love and briefly a single in 1978. EMI withdrew it instead of pushing it, but maybe with New Wave and punk hitting then, the timing was off since it's a bit Dylanesque as well. Hunter then played electric piano on two tracks for the band Tuff Darts.

A project eventually released as *The Secret Sessions* (not included on the massive *Stranded In Reality* box set) was a collaborative supergroup effort including Hunter and Ronson; the effort was organised by Corky Laing, ex-Mountain drummer, and Laing and Hunter co-wrote 'I Ain't No Angel', 'Silent Movie', and 'Easy Money' together. In 1978, Corky Laing, acting on a suggestion from his record company, put a 'supergroup' together featuring himself (drums/vocals), Hunter (ex-Mott The Hoople) on keyboards/vocals, Ronson on guitar and Felix Pappalardi (Mountain) on bass. They started recording, but shortly after, the record company lost interest and funding stopped.

A song from the project, 'The Outsider', would appear in a definitive version on the duo's next studio effort.

The demo quality recording 'I Ain't No Angel' was one of the collaborations on The Secret Sessions with the Mountain band.

'Silent Movie' is a love gone wrong type of song in that the couple has nothing to say to one another, as in a silent movie. It is about communication that breaks down.

'Easy Money' is arguably the best on the record, as the remainder tend to be closer to sounding like demos. Lyrically, it is something like Alice and the woman portrayed is either a lady of the evening or simply down on her luck and looking for easy money while she is out on the run. Hunter and Ronson collaborated musically on the remainder of the tracks on the album as well.

One other curious collaboration involving Laing, Ronson, and Ian was workshop tapes recorded with John Cale. Nonetheless, these songs were never released.

Ronson's demand as a producer had him working consistently but underpaid, but as Hunter guided Mick, he was paid more and Ian then played on David Johansen's *In Style* sessions with Ian playing on 'Flamingo Road'.

Chrysalis tapped Hunter to produce Generate X's second LP *Valley Of The Dolls* and 'King Rocker' reached number 11 on the UK Singles Chart in January 1979 and 'Valley Of The Dolls' reached number 23 in April. The album hit number 51 on the UK Albums Chart. Fortuitously, Ian played demos of his recent songwriting for label head Roy Eldridge and he was intrigued.

The importance of collaborations is that it produced one of his better songs, Hunter was regaining his footing, and perhaps most importantly, he was reunited with his best musical partner for one of their finest albums; and, critical for his musical career, one of Ian's best-selling efforts after two poor-selling albums. Hunter wrote all songs except for one co-write.

'Just Another Night' (Hunter/Ronson)
The album starts with a punchy drum intro by Weinberg, Ian's spoken count, and the signature piano flare-up as the song chronicles one of the best-known stories about Ian's storied career. The song is about the 1973 night with Mott The Hoople when he spent a night in the Indianapolis jail after

mouthing off to an off-duty sergeant, an Indiana State Trooper, at a Holiday Inn hotel. Ian resided with a Black Panther staring at him all night while this was their only off-the-road time, and Ariel Bender got to imbibe refreshments and a cosy hotel bed while Ian was preoccupied. Upon release, early the next morning, no one recognised the shadeless Hunter, although court people were talking about their gig.

Ian notes that the song may have been a hit since Roy Bittan, the keyboardist, heard it as a commercial release, but Hunter and Ronson talked him out of it. As an early alternative, a Springsteen-like slow version entitled, 'The Other Side Of Life' could have been a popular hit, but as revved up by Hunter-Ronson, it was less commercial.

The Hunter and Ronson revved-up version provided for a co-writing trade since Ian wanted the scrawled phrase 'You're Never Alone With A Schizophrenic' found on a bog wall at Wessex Sound Studios, the same place Ian produced Billy Idol's Generation X; Mick gave up the phrase for the LP title and earned co-writing credit.

'Wild East'

The slow burn groove of 'Wild East' featured Hoople-style piano chords and blistering sax. It is a mildly energetic and melodic song about the Wild West relocated to New York.

Hunter enjoys writing tales of those who are down and out and here is one such example. It is an ordinary bloke but one with literary references atypical of pop songs. He feels like Jason was sent by Pelias on an impossible mission to fetch the Golden Fleece; along the way, the Cyclops is laughing at him. This guy is a druggie but someone from the methadone clinic calls and says: 'He writes all my lyrics backwards on diapers'.

All this is happening while loving the grease of the Wild East. We see Jezebel, who, along with her husband, instituted the worship of the false gods of Baal and Asherah, talking to Jane. I'd speculate, but maybe this is 'Sweet Jane'.

'Cleveland Rocks'

If not the most representative of Ian's songs, 'Cleveland Rocks' certainly is one of the top three. From the memorable shout start of 'Three! Four!' to the city of inspiration, Cleveland Hunter has expressed his appreciation to those small-town Americans who embraced Mott and the full-tilt rocker has remained a standard of his live act. Towns in middle America support live acts outside the big entertainment areas such as New York or LA. The references are to David Bowie's Jean genies and pop icon James Dean. It's a fun pop song with Mama living in sin and Grandpa as a rocker.

CBS thought that the first version of the song, 'England Rocks', was too regional and wrongly CBS thought it would not sell. As reconstituted, the song honours the city of Cleveland and early rock 'n' roll DJ Alan Freed, who popularised the city as it was considered by the music industry to be a 'breakout' city, where national trends first appeared in a regional market. It has been Hunter's biggest earner as adopted by the *Drew Carey Show*. Freed's announcement fragment beginning the song was taken from an April 1953 archive tape of his *Moondog's Rock 'N' Roll Party* radio show aired on WJW Cleveland. Hunter advises he got the fragment of the idea from the Akron, OH band, Devo. Ronson considerably improved the original version since 'England Rocks' was too heavy on the keyboards with an Earl Slick guitar solo, whereas Ronno layered guitar riffs throughout. And, the repeated 'Ohio' effect on the coda made the track memorable.

'Ships'

'Ships' is one of the most well-known, sensitive, and autobiographical songs in the Hunter catalogue, reprised by 'No Hard Feelings'. The song describes the intense relationship and conflict that he had and worked through with his father, Walter Patterson. Ian understands that his father had a rough life as a soldier, policeman, and in the British Secret Service before a stroke floored him. As a youth, Hunter viewed himself as a typical post-war idiot. The intensity of the conflict lessened as Ian matured and he grasped what his father had to deal with in life.

Musically, there was little chance that they would see eye to eye, but his father appreciated his book *Diary Of A Rock 'N' Roll Star*. His father aspired to be a writer and he was proud of Ian's talent. He even tried to dissect his son's talent in his songwriting. One issue that Father Hunter used was reverse psychology by telling Ian that he would not amount to anything, thinking that would motivate him. The song relates actual events. Hunter bought his parents a Sheltie dog, Kayla, and when she had pups, his parents kept all three. They took walks by the sea in Bispham on the Fylde coast. Both his parents thought Ian more of a writer than a performer, but this song went a long way to mending bridges and his father heard it before his passing at home on Caxton Avenue in Bispham in 1980. Father and son had made peace by then. Ian's mother was a bit miffed since she felt that her family contribution was downplayed and Ian's father got the attention. Nonetheless, Hunter honoured his mother on 'Strings Attached' and with 'All Is Forgiven'. After her husband's passing, Ian's mum moved back to Shropshire.

The song was not easy to write, and it took years to come out. Hunter began the song about the time of the John Cale workshop demos. Ian had the verses but no hook. However, sitting with Max Weinberg, the drummer, one night, he happened to say, 'ships that pass in the night'. It was the original title. That provided Ian with the impetus that he needed to finish the song. Hunter felt the song was just average; however, managers Steve Popovich and Sam Lederman thought more highly of it and encouraged him to finish the song. Good thing he did. The song became a Top Ten cover at number nine by Barry Manilow, with key changes and modulations that had never occurred to Ian. When he was asked if he minded the different musical direction and mellow Manilow covering the song he responded that it made him a pretty penny; there is nothing to complain about that.

'When The Daylight Comes'

'When The Daylight Comes' was released as both an album track and single. Here is a twist on the typical man and woman-together theme. Hunter expresses an overwhelming desire and romantic feeling for the woman, but when the daylight comes, I'll be on my way. Even if they share a bed, he simply wants the intimacy of warmth and care. Usually, a song like this is love 'em and leave 'em, but this is completely unique and tender. Hunter says this sounds like a single, which is the kiss of death. After his experience with Mott The Hoople, Ian thinks his wellspring of hits dried up. The songs that are successful singles are not contrived and seem to spring up organically.

Ronson sang the first two verses of this song and, amusingly, Ian was having a chat with Bruce Springsteen in The Power Station. Mick urged Bruce to sing the song by daring him to sing it, or Ronson would. Sure enough, Mick did the first two verses and Springsteen didn't get to sing it after all. Ian thought Bruce was a nice, humble guy and was surprised when Springsteen asked Hunter about his vocal phrasing since his records sold so much more than Ian's. Hunter wondered why Bruce would even bother asking.

'Life After Death'

'Life After Death' is a bouncy and beautifully produced full-tilt rocker featuring a staccato piano, a memorable drum run, and a fabulous Ronson solo. Hunter could have been reflecting on metaphysical questions, but it may not be quite as existential as the title suggests since Hunter is sorry, smoking so much and feeling the Devil's touch but wondering if he will live. Ian was writing tongue-in-cheek as on 'Wild East'. Feeling under the weather after what sounds like too much partying, he writes a clever line asking: 'I hear choirs filled with Fenders say return to sender'.

Anyone who has partied too hardily can relate to the idea that you might not live.

Hunter relates that this song just came and he did it. The piano track came with a hook and the rest came later about fun and fear.

'Standin' In My Light'

Shimmering keyboards and an atmospheric drone start 'Standin' In My Light' as this song builds once Hunter reveals a new beginning in his life. The entire project started coming together with this song. It is a genuine song about a guy in the way who was a coked-out manager: Fred Heller. And, there are elements of Svengali Tony Defries as well. The song began to take shape after

33

Overnight Angels. Managers have always been difficult for Hunter and this is representative of having issues with them. They want consistency and money. On the other hand, Ian thinks that consistency is boring and the money should be his. The song was tailor-made for Ronson. It began on a keyboard and Ian wrote the song around that sound.

These are the type of people who have their agenda despite the fact that it does not help you. The New York Dolls get a mention since Ian has identified that they could have been much bigger if they had been allowed to develop properly, but they were pushed too hard too early and they should have kept away from dope. Someone was standing in their light as in our own lives; someone can be standing in ours. The trick is to get the naysayers out of the way and find your light.

'Bastard'

'Bastard' is one of the seminal tracks from *Schizophrenic* and one of the most regularly played live songs during the 1979-1980 touring days with Ronson. Ian has said live and in interviews that this is a love song, not like the usual love songs, and his point is that the song is more realistic of actual relationships.

Ian was travelling from Woodstock to his house in Katonah with Mick and Suzi Ronson when the first line arose about 'Vestal Virginia' which led to the development of the entire song. With songwriting, at times, it is the first line that starts the process; with a strong first line, the rest comes easier. To open the track, there is a clever wordplay of 'Vestal Virginia' as a take-off on the Vestal Virgins of ancient Rome. Vesta's acolytes vowed to serve her for at least thirty years, to study and practice her rites in service of the Roman State, and to maintain their chastity throughout. This Virginia is graphically different. A similar reference, of course, is included in Procol Harum's classic 1967 hit, 'A Whiter Shade Of Pale', as 'One of sixteen vestal virgins'. With John Cale's 'eerie, ominous' sound added, Ian thought it was ideal for the tune. Despite Cale's nervousness since he likes to perform live, Ian thought he 'captured the mood and enhanced the track'. The macho-funk in the song is reminiscent of The Rolling Stones' *Black And Blue* era.

'The Outsider'

The new Hunter song 'The Outsider' closes out *Schizophrenic* and is a bit offbeat but still appropriate for Hunter, who does write often of not fitting into society; the difference here is the setting and sounding like it's the Wild, Wild West.

For the final version of the song, Ronson contributes swooping instrumentation paired with beautiful piano and howling prairie wind sounds. The track has noticeable echoes on the drums and vocal tracks while the straightforward recording allowed Ian's strong voice to be added with clarity and charm.

Of this lyric, Hunter thinks the song may have been misdirected to him; it is his Western cowboy star Roy Rogers song. However, he considers that this slow song is one of the three, with 'Ships' and 'Standin' In My Light', that are among the best ballads he's ever written.

Related Songs
'Don't Let Go'
As the project came to a close, Hunter Ronson was tapped to produce Ellen Foley's *Night Out* LP in 1979 and Ian offered her a shelved ballad, 'Don't Let Go'. Hunter wrote the song, but it just didn't fit on *Schizophrenic* with enough ballads already. It sold well for Ellen Foley. It's a straightforward ballad on persevering when the odds are stacked against you.

'Whole Lotta Shakin' Goin' On'
Hunter's tribute to one of his biggest influences, 'Whole Lotta Shakin' Goin' On' is a song associated with Jerry Lee 'The Killer' Lewis. Along with Little Richard, these two early rock 'n' roll pioneers focused the youthful Ian and provided the musical reason for his existence. Along with Chuck Berry and The Everly Brothers, Hunter's path became clearer, first as a fan and then as a performer; music gave Ian his mode of expression.

Hunter saw Jerry Lee at the London Palladium and was amazed. First, the band played without Lewis for forty minutes, then, once on stage, Jerry Lee just combed his hair. The crowd went nuts. He performed only five songs but said, 'I've done all that a man can do' and walked off. Even when Lewis hardly played live, he had that arrogance on stage that Hunter employed in Mott The Hoople and during his solo career. Not surprisingly, one aspect of Ian on stage is his ability to move and mould an audience.

Also, Hunter worked on David Werner's Epic album singing 'High Class Blues' and when Van Morrison was not available, Ian sang a duet with Genya Ravan on 'Junkman'.

Deluxe Edition Track Listing
Disc 1
'Just Another Night'
'Wild East'
'Cleveland Rocks'
'Ships'
'When The Daylight Comes'
'Life After Death'
'Standin' In My Light'
'Bastard'
'The Outsider'
'Don't Let Go' (Demo)
'Ships' (Take 1)

'When The Daylight Comes' (Early Version)
'Just Another Night' (Early Version) (aka 'The Other Side Of Life')
'Whole Lotta Shakin' Goin' On'

Disc 2

'F.B.I'. – Live In Agora Ballroom, Cleveland 18/6/79
'Once Bitten Twice Shy' – Live In Agora Ballroom, Cleveland 18/6/79
'Life After Death' – Live In Agora Ballroom, Cleveland 18/6/79
'Sons And Daughters' – Live At The Hammersmith Odeon, London 22/11/79
'Laugh At Me' – Live At The Hammersmith Odeon, London 22/11/79
'Just Another Night' – Live At The Hammersmith Odeon, London 22/11/79
'One Of The Boys' – Live At The Hammersmith Odeon, London 22/11/79
'Letter To Brittania From Union Jack' – Live In Berkeley Community Theatre, Berkeley 7/7/79
'Bastard' – Live In Berkeley Community Theatre, Berkeley 7/7/79
'All The Way From Memphis' – Live In Agora Ballroom, Cleveland 18/6/79
'Cleveland Rocks' – Live In Agora Ballroom, Cleveland 18/6/79
'All The Young Dudes' – Live At The Hammersmith Odeon, London 22/11/79
'When The Daylight Comes' – Live In Agora Ballroom, Cleveland 18/6/79
'Sweet Angeline' – Live In Agora Ballroom, Cleveland 18/6/7

Conclusion

The project became one of Hunter's most popular releases and received rave reviews on both sides of the pond. Although the singles didn't do so well, American releases of 'Just Another Night' only went to 68 while 'When The Daylight Comes' hit 108. The album entered the UK LP chart on 5 May, staying for three weeks, reaching 49; in the USA, it hit 35 on *Billboard* and charted for twenty-four weeks, which triggered Hunter Ronson to tour for six months. Since the E Street Band was not available, recruits included bassist Martin Bailey, keyboard player Tommy Mandel, guitarist Tommy Morrongiello, keyboards and sax George Meyer, and drummer Hilly Michaels, later Eric Parker when Michaels left. The Ian Hunter Band featuring Mick Ronson embarked on seventy-nine concerts from June to November 1979. Concerts in Chicago and Toronto were filmed for television and they played *The Friday Show* and *Midnight Special*.

A later repackaging of the album included 'Alibi', which is simply a jam and a stream-of-consciousness song. Oddly, Hunter does not even remember recording or singing it!

The late 1970s ended with the infectious energy of Hunter's *You're Never Alone With A Schizophrenic*, but just as the 1970s gave way to the 1980s, Hunter introduced *Welcome To The Club* with the exceptional talent of Ronson on board and an impressive touring band.

Welcome To The Club

Personnel:
Ian Hunter: lead vocals, guitar, piano, harp
Mick Ronson: lead guitar, Moog synthesizer, mandolin, vocals
Tommy Morrongiello: guitar, vocals
Tommy Mandel: keyboards
Martin Briley: bass
Eric Parker: drums
George Meyer: keyboards, vocals, saxophone
Ellen Foley, Susie Ronson: vocals on 'Standin' In My Light'
Recorded at The Roxy Theatre, West Hollywood, CA, by Ian Hunter and Mick Ronson
Release date: 26 March 1980
Running time: 58:38 (Disc 1) 55:40 (Disc 2)
Current edition: Chrysalis
Highest chart places: UK: 61, US: 69

Imagine the scene: Ian Hunter, having completed a period of rest, stands at the precipice of stardom. Triumphantly, with the wind of triumph in his sails, one would assume smooth sailing lay ahead. However, this newfound success posed a curious challenge: how best to channel his creativity? The answer emerged as a dual-purpose endeavour. Hunter unveiled a live album, capturing the raw energy of his electrifying performances while also weaving in a handful of tantalizing studio gems.

Hunter Ronson 'Rocked The Roxy' by playing a week of sold-out shows at the West Hollywood venue. Chrysalis taped six sets from 5-11 November 1979 and broke the record for the most consecutive nights booked at the Sunset Boulevard club. The first announced title was 'From The Knees Of My Heart' (dropped then, but the phrase would be reprised), but it would be released under the final title instead. Not everyone was thrilled among the Hollywood celebrities because Hunter heard Cher walk out one night after hearing 'Laugh At Me'. Hunter Ronson also performed dates in England and they found enthusiastic crowds and received positive press.

Otherwise, Ian kept busy while mixing the live album. Hunter helped out fellow management act, The Iron City Houserockers, on the *Have A Good Time But Get Out Alive!* album. Ian contributed instrumentation, backing vocals, and production on two tracks. Hunter also produced a single 'Dangerous Eyes' for Sam the Band. Songs previously covered from other albums are not listed. Hunter wrote all songs for the release unless otherwise noted.

'FBI' (Hank Marvin/Bruce Welch/Jet Harris)
This is a showcase for Ronson and opened the Hunter Ronson concerts from 1979-1980. It was a 1961 hit for the Shadows actually written by the band, but due to complicated publishing contracts, it was credited to their manager,

Peter Gormley. Ian didn't particularly care for the Shadows (he 'always took the piss out of him [Ronson] for it at every opportunity'), but Ronno really liked them, made the tune his own, and he added blistering solos to the original and mixed it up a bit.

'Sweet Angeline'

'Sweet Angeline' – sometimes shortened to just 'Angeline' – was a favourite performed live and was originally released on Mott The Hoople's *Brain Capers*. It's a great up-tempo rocker and was highlighted during the 1979-1980 shows. Hunter likes to perform it on occasion, reminding him of producer Guy Stevens. He plays harp in an unusual way for the song; he blows instead of sucks and Ian says it's like reading newspapers backwards.

'Laugh At Me' (Sonny Bono)

Sonny Bono's 'Laugh at Me'– originally issued by Sonny & Cher on their second full-length album in 1966, but without vocals from Cher – was certainly instrumental in Ian's career since he sang it while auditioning for Mott The Hoople. He openly admired Bono's less-than-stellar singing style. Hunter can relate to the song as people used to laugh at him. He wore shades before it was fashionable and people associated sunglasses with having a big head and Hunter admits he does. Ian gives off an arrogant vibe and that's how he likes it. The lyrics fit Hunter as he felt like an outsider growing up. A story is told that may be apocryphal, but Cher supposedly heard the song in 1979 at the Roxy in LA and disliked it so much that she walked out.

'All The Way From Memphis'

'All The Way From Memphis' is one of Ian's most well-known tunes from both the studio release and his live concerts. It is a homage to rock 'n' roll roots from Memphis and, in the piano intro, especially to The Killer, Jerry Lee Lewis. During gig performances, Ian has said live that the original rock and roller Jerry Lee Lewis told him there is only one thing to do when the music is low; you have to turn the sound up again! How appropriate it is that Sun Records signed Ian with *Defiance Part 1*, as he also recorded 'Ghosts' as a tribute to early rock 'n' roll and the city of Memphis.

The song is mostly true and based on the 1972 Mott The Hoople concert in Memphis. This was Ian's famous invasion of Graceland that he relates in *Diary Of A Rock 'N' Roll Star*. The foray didn't prove entirely successful, but Ian got the song out of the experience.

Hunter was not happy with the 'Memphis' mix from *Mott,* so he was happy to do it again and perform it live as well. Understandably, Ian objected to the Mott version as a single, but the CBS UK Head Dick Asher put it out as soon as Hunter's back was turned on a US tour. It went Top Ten. Ian says he can be a poor judge of his own work.

The track was originally a Mott The Hoople song but Ian has consistently performed it live in concert officially from 1979-2004. It has become a staple of his live act as he moves to the piano while playing it live. The studio version relates 'she rides the train to Oreoles' (or Oriole), but when Luther Grosvenor (aka Ariel Bender) played in the band, Ian substituted 'Ariel' for 'Oreoles', otherwise he sings the original version. The Liverpool Docks and the Oreoles were poetic license. Some of the lyrics are true, and some fictionalised. Over the years, Hunter also changed the politically incorrect 'spade', a mildly derogatory word for a black male, to the neutral word dude.

More importantly, the song is a paean to the aspirations and the desperation of rockers seeking success. Hunter references the Beatles, 'From the Liverpool Docks to the Hollywood Bowl', noting their origin and their famous Bowl appearance, insightfully identifying a rocker's internal thoughts of pursuing success at any cost, 'As your name gets hot, so your heart grows cold. 'N you gotta stay young man, you can never be old'. Age is something Ian understands first-hand since early in his career; he struggled to be in the band Mott The Hoople at the old age, at least for rock, of 29 years old. Hunter also lamented the coldness of the music business, most famously in his *Diary Of A Rock 'N' Roll Star*. He also consistently identified the limitation of stardom in *Diary* and elsewhere as in his lyric: "N you look like a star but you're really out on parole!' As Hunter has struggled for recognition he popped the bubble off the rock lifestyle since it was not all that it was cracked up to be. You may be in a band, on tour, and recording, but you are not making any money. More than anyone else in the history of popular music, Ian has honestly revealed what the rock lifestyle is really like.

'I Wish I Was Your Mother'
Originally, 'I Wish I Was Your Mother' was the closing track on the Mott The Hoople *Mott* release and later popped up throughout Ian's solo career. One thought at the time of the original release is that the song is one of the most personal Hunter songs, not a band track, and not surprisingly, he has returned to it during his solo releases. The lyrics are highly personal to Ian and his frustration of not having an ideal upbringing. The song was prompted by his wife's more normal family and his desire to have experienced a better childhood with parents and siblings. The song is about heavy jealousy. People warned others about a troubled Hunter with his unhealthy background, most notably Trudi's own mother who, when she heard the song, exclaimed: 'get rid of him'.

'Walkin' With A Mountain'
The 'Walkin' With a Mountain' rocker was released on *Mad Shadows* and is an up-tempo song with a segue into The Rolling Stones track 'Jumpin' Jack Flash'. The original release for Mott The Hoople needed something fast and the song was written in about ten minutes. In Olympic Studios, Guy Stevens

said a rocker was needed, so Ian immediately launched into this two-chord, obvious song and Stevens was delighted. Mick Ralphs wrote 'Rock and Roll Queen' on demand for the band in 1969 and this one came similarly. One day, Hunter saw a guy leaning up against a lamp post on his bike with a little radio strapped to his crossbar listening to 'Half Moon Bay' which inspired Ian. Another related memory for Hunter was a letter to *Rolling Stone* claiming that Bob Dylan was trying to sound like Mott. Early on, Mott didn't think that highly of themselves, but these songs were inspiring chaps and rockers such as this are the result.

'All The Young Dudes' (David Bowie)
The most well-known of all Mott The Hoople songs, 'All The Young Dudes' is closely associated with Ian. Originally released as a Mott song, it has continued to be a staple of Hunter's live shows from 1979-2010. The widely circulated story is that Mott broke up and Pete 'Overend' Watts rang Bowie up to see if he needed a bass player. Instead, David said he was a fan and had material for Mott, thus first, Overend and then the whole band went to his flat to hear songs. The band needed a killer song to break into the charts and Ian said he knew it was a hit the first time he heard it; this effort was their last grasp at commercial success and it did break them into the charts. The ending rap was uncredited to Ian from a stage prank that he pulled on stage wherein he would invite someone from the audience to come forward or pour beer over them. Nonetheless, he did not get songwriting credit as it was originally Bowie's song. Hunter's pop instincts were keen, though and he turned down David's first offering of 'Suffragette City' and the band readily embraced 'All The Young Dudes' as a result.

'Slaughter On Tenth Avenue' (Richard Rodgers)
This is a Ronson solo track from his solo album *Slaughter On Tenth Avenue,* but also released on *Welcome To The Club* and there is also a live version from the Rockpalast show in 1980. The song was included on Ronson's first LP when David Bowie came in with his crowd and just took over. Bowie ran out of time, although he promised to write lyrics for the tune. As they ran out of time, Mick asked about the words, but he responded he didn't feel like writing and wandered off. Ronson finished the song alone in two days without Bowie and without lyrics; this is a classy all-guitar track and featured live touring as the Hunter Ronson Band.

'We Gotta Get Outta Here'
One of the few new songs on the CD is 'We Gotta Get Outta Here' about the New York Club scene. The critique is two-sided: one for the hapless crowd who is attracted to the dead-end clubs and the other target is the gossip mongers who celebrate the degenerates who frequent the establishments. The song may have targeted Studio 54 since Hunter went to it only once. The

timing was right for satire since the disco fad was at its height. Ian did like Donna Summer, though.

It was an attempt at a single and in retrospect, Hunter is not too fond of the attempt. He has said singles just come organically and they are more inspired. The band had been off the road for six weeks and at first tried to record at My Father's Place in Roslyn, New York, which didn't work, so they went back to try again by recording live in the studio.

'Silver Needles'

'Silver Needles' could be about almost any victim of the rock star lifestyle, so speculation has centred on who it could be about. Silver needles are the downfall of so many stars in the limelight; Hunter is saying he understands the pressure that public figures experience, but he is not dead and is still standing. Ian identifies that the song is loosely based on Deep Purple guitarist Tommy Bolin, who did not heed Hunter's advice after he had signed a book for him. Bolin died in 1976 from an overdose of heroin and other substances, including alcohol, cocaine, and barbiturates. Ian adds that it might have Sid Vicious in mind as well since he passed away in February 1979, someone else who died but believed what the music papers said about him. He thinks that the papers should mirror and not lead music. For example, if the New York Dolls had not been pushed out too soon, stayed away from drugs, and allowed to develop, they would have been more long-lasting.

'Man O' War' (Hunter/Ronson)

This song is so blatant and misogynist, unlike almost anything Ian has written; I would suspect there is a bit of fun going on here. It's a tongue-in-cheek, twelve-bar, Stones-style rocker. It's as if Ian is pulling our leg because the lyrics are so comical; I mean, 'demon of the semen', seriously? Hunter openly states he and Ronson weren't keen on the song after having been on the road so much he had just about hit empty. He was desperate to write in San Diego for a week where they were rehearsing for the Roxy week dates. They needed almost anything, and this is the result. It's sort of like a perverse pleasure to hear something so wooden, but after repeated plays, the song grows on you.

'Sons And Daughters'

'Sons And Daughters' is a country-style ballad and an autobiographical tale about Hunter's divorce, living near the Archway in London, and losing contact with both his first son and his daughter. The song is reminiscent of 'Waterlow'. Ian worked semi-skilled factory work at the capstans, which is a vertical-axle rotating machine developed for use on sailing ships to multiply the pulling force of seamen when hauling ropes, cables, and hawsers (thick cable or rope). Hunter worked at British Timken, which was a big engineering firm making screws, nuts and bolts.

Once Hunter was pursuing music seriously, he divorced his first wife Diane and made both of his children, Stephen and Tracie, lonely when he left. He recognised the damage he'd caused and he found a band, Mott The Hoople, to go out on tour. Stars are fools, he says. He remarries Trudi, who may want children as well and as a result, the nightmare returns like a ghost if he repeats the mistake of the past. The song is about guilt and pain and all is true in Ian's case. He says you can never put it right.

'One Of The Boys' (Hunter/Ralphs)

The Mick Ralphs and Hunter song 'One Of The Boys' was originally from the *All The Young Dudes* LP and played on the 1979 tour as well as being released on a 2002 version. Most of the *Welcome* LP is from the Sunday night show at the Roxy in LA. As a result of having too much solid material, 'Boys' was cut, as well as crowd responses. Ralphs began the song in 1971, but Hunter couldn't sing 'Can't Get Enough', so the same riff is used in 'Boys' for the *Dudes* LP and Mick got credit for writing half the song. Ralphs finished the original later and had a huge hit with Bad Company. 'Boys' as a song is probably more indicative of Mott The Hoople as a band than 'Dudes' is. The live song version was so dynamic that Eric Parker actually left his drum stool on the song.

'The Golden Age Of Rock 'N' Roll'

There are several songs that Ian has written that celebrate rock 'n' roll, and as on *The Hoople* LP, they work well as opening tracks. 'The Golden Age Of Rock 'N' Roll' also opened their live shows, whereas in his solo career, the song appears mid-set. In 1973, there was a furore about noise levels at rock concerts – the 96 decibel freaks – about the time the song was written. As performed during Ian's solo career the song celebrated the fun times he had as a singer with a band. Hunter resurrected this tune on the 1979 tour; it was very much a band effort reminding Ian of the Mott The Hoople days.

CD Reissue
Disc 1
'F.B.I'. (Hank Marvin, Bruce Welch, Jet Harris) (3:51)
'Once Bitten, Twice Shy' (5:25)
'Angeline' (4:56)
'Laugh At Me' (Sonny Bono) (3:40)
'All The Way From Memphis' (3:33)
'I Wish I Was Your Mother' (6:47)
'Irene Wilde' (4:13)
'Just Another Night' (Hunter, Mick Ronson) (6:03)
'Cleveland Rocks' (6:01)
'Standin' In My Light' (5:49)
'Bastard' (8:12)

Disc 2
'Walking With A Mountain/Rock 'N' Roll Queen' (Hunter, Mick Ralphs) (4:19)
'All The Young Dudes' (David Bowie) (3:30)
'Slaughter On Tenth Avenue' (Richard Rodgers) (2:25)
'One Of The Boys' (Hunter, Ralphs) (7:36)
'The Golden Age Of Rock 'N' Roll' (4:01)
'When The Daylight Comes' (9:00)
'Medley: Once Bitten Twice Shy/Bastard/Cleveland Rocks' (6:10)
'We Gotta Get Out Of Here' (3:14)
'Silver Needles' (5:56)
'Man O' War' (Hunter, Ronson) (4:19)
'Sons And Daughters' (5:04)

Conclusion
The album entered the British chart on 26 April and remained for two weeks. It is a tribute to the longest tour Hunter has ever been on and represents his 1970s repertoire, with a full-on rocking set blending both Mott and solo classics, with a few twists, and clever rapport thrown in for good measure. It demonstrates how well Hunter and Ronson seamlessly worked live with a great and well-rehearsed band. The critics generally praised the effort.

A British promo in a limited edition brushed America's Top 100 chart. Chrysalis promoted a three-track video featuring Ellen Foley and the audio included 'Irene Wilde', 'Once Bitten Twice Shy', 'We Gotta Get Out Of Here' and 'Slaughter On 10th Avenue'. Additional promotion included a gig in April 1980 at the Rockpalast, the German music showcase. The set was recorded on 19 April at Grugahalle Arena in Essen. The gig was released as *Live At Rockpalast: The Ian Hunter Band Featuring Mick Ronson* in 2012.

A repackaging of *Welcome To The Club* in 1983 and 1994 as *Ian Hunter Live* addressed some of the issues of the original release. There were previously unreleased live takes and a bluesy ten-minute-plus version of 'When The Daylight Comes'. On 'The Golden Age Of Rock 'N' Roll', there is a fun doo-wop middle eight, an introductory a cappella section, and, as Ian introduced, 'a little bit of New York City toilet music'.

Later, in May and June, Hunter Ronson embarked on an American tour. But a big change was not long in coming. The pair was having fun, but prior to the Dr Pepper concert in New York, Mick announced he was leaving. The remaining gigs were cancelled and the band folded.

Hunter assembled a new band for a video performance that was released as *Ian Hunter Rocks*. It was so hot Ian felt his knees buckle and had to leave the stage once to catch his breath. Then, at New York's Palladium Theatre on 13 September, Ian appeared at 'The Party at the Palladium' charity concert for fellow musician Rick Derringer when he had his musical equipment stolen; the concert was released as *King Biscuit Flower Hour Presents Rick Derringer*

And Friends In Concert featuring a blistering 'Just Another Night' and a medley of Mott and Ian solo songs.

In the interim before the next album, a new song, 'Lullaby', Hunter offered to Tommy Mandel for a Cleveland International charity album, *Children Of The World*. More importantly, the non-political Ian agreed to play twelve charity concerts with Todd Rundgren in support of Congressman John Anderson, who was an independent candidate in the 1980 US presidential election. Ian brought Tommy Mandel to join in Rundgren's assemblage billed as 'An Evening with Todd Rundgren and Ian Hunter'. The group played several of Ian's songs and covers. Ronson joined for a Cleveland concert. Hunter also gigged with Todd for a benefit for Vietnam Vets. Ian also appears in a 90-minute Rundgren film entitled *The Ever Popular Tortured Artist Effect*.

Hunter was at the top of his game and his last studio and live album celebrated his success. Naturally, Chrysalis craved another studio LP to cash in on Ian's popularity. Hunter started recording 'Theatre Of The Absurd', a title later abandoned, but the title did reappear as a song later; in any case, the next studio effort would both be a surprise for his fans and also a shock for Chrysalis.

Ian Hunter surpasses the limitations of his highly acclaimed previous studio album, *You're Never Alone With A Schizophrenic,* and ventures into uncharted sonic territory with the enigmatic new studio release *Short Back 'N' Sides*. Hunter reinvents himself, embracing an eclectic blend of new wave, pop, and daring experimentation. Collaborating with visionary Mick Jones as the producer and Ronson on guitar, Hunter revealed his vulnerable depths of 'Rain' to the irresistible allure of 'Theatre Of The Absurd', with an unyielding commitment to pushing the boundaries of his art. Experimentation abounded with a double CD with thirteen extra tracks and different mixes.

Short Back 'N' Sides

Personnel:
Ian Hunter: lead vocals, guitars, piano
Mick Ronson: lead guitar, keyboards, vocals
Tommy Mandel: keyboards
Tommy Morrongiello: bass, vocals
Martin Briley: bass
Eric Parker: drums
George Meyer: keyboards, vocals
Mick Jones: guitars, vocals
Topper Headon: drums, percussion
Tymon Dogg: violin
Ellen Foley: vocals
Miller Anderson: vocals
Mick Baraken: guitar on 'Gun Control'
Wells Kelly: drums on 'Gun Control'
John Holbrook: bass on 'Gun Control'
Gary Windo: alto saxophone on 'I Need Your Love'
Roger Powell: backing vocals on 'I Need Your Love'
Todd Rundgren: bass, backing vocals on 'I Need Your Love'
Produced at: The Power Station, Wizard Sound and Electric Lady Studios, New Youk, and Wessex Studio London by Mick Jones and Mick Ronson
Release date: 29 August 1981
Running time: 44:55 (Original release) 105:38 (2 CD edition)
Current edition: Chrysalis
Highest chart places: UK: 79, US: 62

The next release of Hunter's oeuvre is audacious. As Hunter himself boldly declares, 'I don't say much, but I make a big noise'. In 1981, *Short Back 'N' Sides* was a curious offering that would leave fans divided and intrigued in equal measure. But amidst the musical whirlwind, a precious gift arrived: the birth of his son, John Jesse Hunter Patterson, an event that added an extra layer of profundity to his artistic journey.

With Ronson at the production helm, aided by the likes of Martin Briley, Tommy Mandel, Tommy Morrongiello, Eric Parker, and George Meyer, the recording process embarked upon a tumultuous path. As the studio days stretched on, a momentary lull in enthusiasm prompted Hunter and Ronson to seek assistance, and lo and behold, who should answer the call but the fervent Mott devotee himself, Mick Jones of The Clash.

Yet, even with the injection of fresh energy, Hunter candidly admits that venturing into uncharted musical territories can be a double-edged sword. The creative well running dry, Ronson gracefully stepped aside, allowing Jones to take the reins for the remainder of the endeavour. With Jones's inventive prowess, the sonic tapestry morphed into a kaleidoscope of odd sound effects and a captivating amalgamation of genres. It was, without a doubt, the most daring and experimental venture Hunter had ever embarked upon previously – a testament to the boundless depths of his artistic exploration. Immerse yourselves in a sonic odyssey that defies convention and challenges expectations about the artist that is Ian Hunter.

All songs were written by Ian Hunter except where noted.

'Central Park 'N' West'

This opening track stands up well despite a mixed response to this LP overall mostly as a result of Mick Jones' production. There were sound effects Jones added and different production techniques which didn't always serve the song, but on this track, the added elements work.

The song seems firmly ensconced in New York City and refers to the Central Park West Historic District between the 61st and 97th Streets of the title. Ian and Ronson lived in the Mayflower Hotel for six months and its residents have included actors, athletes, CEOs, hedge fund managers, entrepreneurs, and musicians, including Sting. The song is Ian's attempt to say something good about the City when it was slagged in the English press and the lyrics came to him one night when he was looking out of a ninth-floor window. It was originally a poem, and Jones liked the lyrics and wrote some chords for it, including lots of little sounds that Ian says he never would have thought of.

The landmarks of Central Park and West include the Dakota, gaining infamy when resident John Lennon was shot dead outside the building on 8 December 1980. Ian mentions listening to Frank Carillo, who is an American rock musician, perhaps best known from a band called Doc Holliday. You have to be crazy to live in New York City, but still, it's the best, which is probably Ian's own reflections on the city, having been a resident himself. He really catches the vibe and energy of the city with its music, waitresses, and 'soul woman'.

'Lisa Likes Rock 'N' Roll'

Often, there is a funny, comical, or humorous song on releases and 'Lisa Likes Rock 'n' Roll' is a good example of one, but it also has the cuteness factor going for it; also, references in the song can be understood as one of Ian's tributes to rock 'n' roll. 'Wango-tango' is a song by rocker Ted Nugent and a music series by LA radio station KIIS-FM, 'Peppermint' was a popular NYC discotheque open from 1958-1965 and the launchpad for the global Twist craze, 'Be-Bop-a-Lula' is a rockabilly song recorded in 1956 by Gene Vincent and His Blue Caps, while 'Peggy Sue' was released by Buddy Holly in 1957.

The cuteness is supplied with the saying 'You're my daddy', difficult to get but finally said by Ronson's daughter, four or five-year-old Lisa. The song has been described as carrying the radiator and tin-can rattle of Bo Diddley. The Ronsons lived with the Hunters part of the time and Ian wrote this kid's song for her, but it was not easy to get her to say the phrase correctly. The families were so close that if anything had happened to Mick and Suzi Ronson, the Hunters would have taken her in. Ian relates that he knew he was taking a chance with a fun song like this: easy for The Rolling Stones to do but a chance to take for a lesser-known artist such as Hunter.

'I Need Your Love'

Regardless of the production issues, the lyrics of 'I Need Your Love' are heartfelt and contrite from the lack of love in life. The singer is expressive, tender, and freely desires love for someone who breaks through his coldness. Hunter feels that the song never really made it. He thinks it is dreary, but he persisted at the time; the drums and bass have no spark and it didn't sound like Ian heard it in his head. Perhaps surprisingly, the single went Top 50 in one American chart.

'Old Records Never Die'

'Old Records Never Die' is about music that touches us deeply and does not let go. Often, when you hear a song, it takes you to a special time or moment that you will never forget. This song started as more of a general commentary about Elvis Presley, but in NYC, John Lennon was shot while the song was being recorded at The Power Station. Hunter recognised a reporter from Channel 7 that he knew. Producer Bob Clearmountain and the musicians were stunned, but Ian seized the moment and was inspired to do more while outside people reacted and were horrified by the tragedy. The assassin at The Dakota was wearing a Todd Rundgren *Hermit Of Mink Hollow* T-shirt when he was arrested. Hunter feels the song has a good hook but should have harmonies on the hook. It could have been a hit and Ian singles out the magnificent Tommy Mandel on keyboards for this track. Mandel adds that the band was walking back to The Mayflower from the Power Station at what at the time was Roosevelt Hospital. They had just recorded the album version of 'Old Records Never Die'.

'Noises' (Ian Hunter/Tommy Morrongiello)

'Noises' has a reference to *Waiting For Godot* by Samuel Beckett, but mostly, there is a great deal of wordplay throughout. It started as a poem and without Mick Jones producing, Ian said the song might not have seen the light of day. He arranged the start-stop at the beginning, whereas Hunter wrote the song with Tommy Morrongiello (guitar, bass). They had a great deal of fun with it, but the two cents of former producer Guy Stevens was to cut off the pretentious intro.

'Rain'

'Rain' is a peaceful, rolling and hypnotic ballad about Ian's youth. Hunter has managed to write emotional songs about his life and, in particular, his youth between the ages of 16 and 27 and this is one of his most heartfelt. This is about his Northampton period and rain is a metaphor for the difficulty, violence, and poverty that afflicted the town. He names his mates – Barry Parkes, Johnny Facer, Tony Perrett, and Alan Manship – and their depressing prospects, including those who are no longer with us, 'Biddy' didn't make it and passed at 23 years old. Ian got out, but I suppose it was not easy since his prospects, like his mates were not promising. Hunter was living a life as a journeyman worker until he broke out of a dead-end life with his musical talent. Ian says this period of his life is still very much with him.

'Gun Control'
Musically upbeat, the satirical 'Gun Control' had clear targets. Hunter has consistently expressed reservations about guns and the NRA and this is his strongest statement to that effect and is more directly political than most of his songs. He expressed the same anger against stupidity from his first solo album about his first reaction to America and here picks up the theme. The context is really the United States since he refers to the president, not long after the attempt on Ronald Reagan's life, Washington, and the Constitution. Hunter includes the sarcastic 'viva macho' associating guns with machismo and the song was a part of his standard live set in 1981.

'Theatre Of The Absurd'
The LP was not always well received, but the only attempt at a reggae-flavoured song is 'Theatre Of The Absurd'. The song lived up to its promise. This is a song about Brixton and the fruitful collaboration of rock and reggae as Ian adapted another poem for a musical format. Hunter saw the flowering of mixing two forms of music as early as 1973 and culminated with the Clash. Ian contrasts his rock theatre of the absurd with Jones' music. Neither Ronson nor Hunter understood reggae but leaned on Jones for the effects, sound, and ideas. Belatedly, Hunter thought 'Brixton Rock' would have made a better title and is reminiscent of the Clash's 'Guns Of Brixton'. As Ronson and Hunter were out of ideas, Jones came in and started with this song and his stylings, which stretched to the entire album. At the time, Ian says he and Ronson were bored, idle and lazy, allowing Jones to take creative control.

'Leave Me Alone'
From an album with mixed tracks and problematic production comes 'Leave Me Alone', which is one of those young love ballads that Ian writes consistently. But, there is a twist with this one as the guy desires the girl who teases him because she already has a boyfriend. She's a flirt, so the guy pleads with her to leave him alone. It might have been written for fun.

The song had been around since *Overnight Angels* and was written for airplay, but Ian wishes he had never written it. He tried the same with 'To

Love A Woman' and didn't get either of these two songs right. They both seemed like singles, but neither came off well. This is the problem Ian has expressed elsewhere; if you try to write in an artificial manner, the songs don't come off, but strong songs and singles are similar to gifts. They just come direct.

'Keep On Burning'

'Keep On Burning' closes out the album, originally entitled 'Burning Bridges', and the chorus rocks, providing a strong ending for the sequence of songs. Ian expresses admiration for gospel, although he says the style is alien to him; however, the tune does build to a gospel-like frenzy. Hunter cites his love of Leon Russell's playing and the ending sounds like it could be him. And, despite the limitations expressed about the production of the album and Hunter describing this effort as an 'odd' track, this song is one that can stand on its own as a strong effort. It is a reflection on current love.

Related Songs
'Detroit'

The 'Detroit' outtake can actually be found in three versions: a rough mix and instrumental, take one, and a vocal outtake five. The track is from the *Schizophrenic* sessions. It is catchy with a good beat but unfinished and missing full lyrics to fill the track out. It sounds like a work in progress. It is an ode to the American car industry as it was losing its dominance against Japanese competition. Bassist Mark Clarke remembers Hunter lending him the big American car depicted in *Creem* Stars Cars (not the Pinto!) for a couple of days.

'Na Na Na'

'Na Na Na' is a sax workout and a 1950s-style romp inspired by Little Richard. Early in his career, Hunter wrote this song which sounds ideal for the early rock 'n' roller. There were even some words created for this song and Ian says they were good. Hunter openly admires Richard by calling him the Governor, the greatest of all time, and he has the finest natural voice for rock 'n' roll. Paul Rodgers is good as well, but second to Little Richard. Hunter thinks his early bands were incredible and second to none; when Jimi Hendrix was in his band, he told him to cool it. Jimi went on to other famous things.

'I Believe In You'

'I Believe in You' is very rough and nothing more than a working demo.

'Listen To The Eight Track'

Songs like 'Listen To The Eight Track' do not happen often but it reminds me of Guy Stevens when he provoked a stream-of-consciousness groove as on 'I Can Feel'. Hunter loves this track, including the boomerang at the end.

49

'You Stepped Into My Dreams'

'You Stepped Into My Dreams' is strong and a just miss for inclusion on the album. In a way, this song is similar to 'Arms And Legs' since, despite the strong feeling of love, this might be about the one that got away. The guy is leaving since:

> We both gotta be moving on
> Sometimes you see a lover and she's made for love
> But you let that lover slip by
> You believe and yet she's so hard to get
> And you never know the reasons why

He is clearly enamoured, but he's getting on a plane, maybe never to return, although she stepped into his dreams.

'Venus In The Bathtub'

This one never made it since the band didn't get the groove.

'China'

'China' could be emotional for Ian now that Ronson passed, but Hunter had Ronno sing it at the time because it's a trawler boat song similar to Mick's hometown of Hull. Mick is still with us.

1995 Bonus CD (Long Odds And Outtakes)

'Detroit' (Rough Mix – Instrumental) (3:42)
'Na Na Na' (4:13)
'I Need Your Love' (Rough Mix) (3:46)
'Rain' (Alternative Mix) (5:50)
'I Believe In You' (4:15)
'Listen To The Eight Track' (6:08)
'You Stepped Into My Dreams' (4:41)
'Venus In The Bathtub' (4:29)
'Theatre Of The Absurd' (6:08)
'Detroit' (Outtake 5 – Vocal) (4:00)
'Na Na Na' (Extended Mix) (4:29)
'China' (Mick Ronson Vocal) (4:36)
'Old Records Never Die' (Version 1) (4:18)

Conclusion

The experiment spent eleven weeks on *Billboard* in the US. The single was 'Lisa Likes To Rock 'N' Roll' with the B-side 'Noises' released as a clear vinyl pressing. 'Central Park 'N' West' and 'I Need Your Love' were released variously as A-sides in Europe and America, the latter hit number 47 on one US chart.

Almost surprisingly, many critics responded positively to Jones' trick fade-outs, odd percussion, weird sounds, and liberal use of echo.

For many fans, though, this was Hunter's least approachable effort and an ambitious, unfocused stylistic experiment was not to their taste. Ian feels the experiment was akin to a garage album, which can indeed work as on *Ian Hunter's Dirty Laundry*. Hunter was distracted by Trudi's pregnancy and the interesting work was not pleasing to his label or his manager, who ignored him. Musically, Ronson had checked out and Hunter formed a new band to promote the record.

As a new band was being formed, it was an unsettled time and on 29 August 1981, the tragic news broke that original Mott The Hoople mentor Guy Stevens passed away from an accidental overdose of a prescribed drug. Hunter was moved by his earliest musical supporter and wrote a 1981 poem about him to include as verse in the artwork for his next album.

The new band had been assembled for the 11 September Dr Pepper Festival and consisted of Tommy Mandel, keyboards, drummer Mark Kaufman, guitarist Robbie Alter, and bassist Mark Clarke. They played on 8 August 1981 at the Milton Keynes Bowl while Thin Lizzy's Phil Lynott babysat with their newborn son, Jesse; one other gig was at the 101 Club in South London. Ronson did appear with the band at gigs when keyboardist Mandel was hospitalised.

As the Ian Hunter Band, in January 1982, they played the Old Waldorf in San Francisco, which was broadcast by the Westwood One radio network, and Don Kirchner's Rock Concert playing Dylan's 'Is Your Love In Vain' from his recent *Street Legal* release. They also participated in the Concert for Vietnam Veterans Agency Orange Victims. Hunter began writing 'Absent Friends' and 'You're Messin' With The King Of Rock 'N' Roll'.

After an audacious release, Ian Hunter takes us on a captivating transition from the daring sonic landscapes of *Short Back 'N' Sides* to the infectious allure of *All Of The Good Ones Are Taken*. Like a master storyteller, Hunter weaves a musical narrative that traverses the realms of rock, pop, and timeless melodies. With his signature wit and charm, he invites us into a world where love, longing and self-discovery intertwine. From the electrifying energy of 'Something's Goin' On' to the heartfelt introspection of 'All Of The Good Ones Are Taken', each track unveils a new layer of Hunter's artistry. Collaborating with a team of exceptional musicians, he crafts a sound that is both nostalgic and contemporary, blending catchy hooks, soul-filled harmonies, and infectious rhythms. Hunter ignites with his timeless melodies and undeniable charisma, proving once again that he is a true icon of rock.

All Of The Good Ones Are Taken

Personnel:
Ian Hunter: lead vocals, guitar, piano
Mick Ronson: lead guitar on 'Death 'N' Glory Boys'
Robbie Alter: guitar, vocals
Tommy Mandel: keyboards
Bob Mayo: keyboards
Hilly Michaels: drums
Mark Clarke: bass guitar, vocals
Clarence Clemons: tenor saxophone on 'All Of Good Ones Are Taken' (slow & fast versions) and 'Seeing Double'
Louis Cortelezzi: alto saxophone
Dan Hartman: bass guitar on 'Speechless'
Jeff Bova: keyboards on 'Speechless'
Jimmy Ripp: guitars on 'All Of The Good Ones Are Taken' and 'That Girl Is Rock 'N' Roll'
Rory Dodd: backing vocals on 'All Of The Good Ones Are Taken'
Eric Troyer: backing vocals on 'All Of The Good Ones Are Taken'
Produced at Wizard Sound, New York, by Ian Hunter and Max Norman
Release date: September 1983
Running time: 40:38
Current edition: Columbia
Highest chart places: US: 125

Despite his previous album's mixed reception, numerous record labels sought his services. In 1982, Hunter reunited with Columbia Records, crafting the tracks for his forthcoming release. While two of his initial compositions were left behind, the album boasted a fresh array of tracks, including two collaborative efforts with the likes of Mark Clarke and Hilly Michaels. Hunter fearlessly tackled a myriad of subjects, from the haunting spectre of nuclear missiles to the echoes of the Falklands War. Hunter's sound became sharper, the melodies brighter, and a distinct commercial polish adorned each and every track.

All songs were written by Ian Hunter except where noted.

'All Of The Good Ones Are Taken' (Fast Version)

One of the most attractive new songs, 'All Of The Good Ones Are Taken' featured an infectious chorus and heartfelt sax from Clarence 'The Big Man' Clemons of the E Street Band. Similar to Springsteen's work, this track is one of several in the Hunter oeuvre that has emerged substantially different in more than one version: in this case, a fast and a slow version. The slow version was the first and Ian wanted it for the album, but CBS objected to its release as a single. The fast version was the record company's idea. It was written quickly, but the original was lost and Ian couldn't get the groove for the song back. His wife warned him not to do the fast version and she is correct; the slow version makes it. Ian thinks that he missed out on a hit with the song. It very well could have been a smash since it's a great track.

Similar to the dilemma with 'Just Another Night' and 'The Other Side Of Life' on *You're Never Alone With A Schizophrenic,* ideas were bandied about whether to do the songs fast or slow. On the studio album, the lively, up-tempo version began as the first track and the slow version closed out the effort. The feeling is bittersweet – lost love – the feeling at the end of a romance, that's it.

Furthermore, we have the treat of a clever, fully-produced music video for the effort as well. The video is a spoof on the actor Dudley Moore in 1981's comedy *Arthur*. The promo video was a superb marketing tool of the time, converting Hollywood visuals into a three-minute rock expression. The 385-pound late Captain Haggerty from his 'School for Dogs' and television's Mr. Clean helped Ian through the shoot with his encouragement. During the Central Park boat scene, the craft sinks under the Captain's weight, covering their feet in water and waterlogging the cassette needed for the lip-synching. Hunter was soaked for the limousine scene and the diner shot required a 4 am shoot so they could open up for business that morning. In 1984 the clip was nominated at the first-ever MTV Video Music Awards.

'Every Step Of The Way' (Hunter/Clarke)
'Every Step Of The Way' is a simple love song which has a basic beat and rhythm driving direct verses along with a rolling swath of pop-styled, synth-based choruses. One of the best quotes about this song comes from Ian himself, who has said it is a 'smutty, dumb, love song, but good dumb, like 'Woolly Bully' (the 1964 Sam The Sham & The Pharaohs song). It is totally commercial, and not surprisingly, The Monkees recorded their nearly identical version, although with poppier vocals. It is really silly with a line such as 'You sewed a button on my shirt one day' and then he follows the girl 'every step of the way'. Bassist Mark Clarke earned a co-writing credit on the song as well.

'Fun' (Hunter/Clarke/Michaels)
'Fun' is an odd piece and is intricate and bumpy while mixed with guitar riffs, horn sounds, and a cute spoken middle-eight. The song has a hint of desperation as we think we are supposed to have fun even though these days, it is not like the enjoyable things we did in the past. Fun may not be all that much fun after all. It seems to be a song that suggests we need to go out and have a good time even when fun may not be in the offing. Mark Clarke, bass, and Hilly Michaels, drums, get co-songwriting credit on this tune.

'Speechless'
Bassist Dan Hartman of the Edgar Winter Group contributed a great deal to 'Speechless', which is an effective satirical take on obsession and the

absurdity of TV. This is one of the strongest tracks on the record and it was later recorded by Status Quo as well, although their version sounds formulaic. The song seems addressed to a specific person who is so intoxicated they have to be switched off. Hunter confesses that people like this leave him speechless. They got to him and he has to get them off his chest; these are powerful words and filled with emotional weight. Ian is warning about people you're fed up with and, with television, people wasting more time. Kids are passively mesmerised by television, which dumbs us down, and is getting worse. The song is ahead of its time with social media, computers, and the internet. Things have certainly gotten much worse than when this was written in the 1980s. Worse than gross, indeed.

Hunter also played this on stage during the summer of 1991 with The Mats Ronander Band and Swedish covers group The Few.

'Death 'N' Glory Boys'

This is a political song and a straightforward denunciation of the stupidity of continually sending the young off to war. It should be clear that the song is inspired by the trauma of war and Ian has confirmed that the song is about the Falkland Islands war and Prime Minister Margaret Thatcher's adventurism. The conflict cost a great deal of money and young lives, but the song can be applied to any unnecessary warfare. Hunter's daughter was seventeen years old then, which hit home for him that a child that young could be killed in war.

Fortunately, since, on most of the record he is absent, Ronson offered a blistering guitar solo with Ian next to him. Hunter reports that Ronno forgot the chords, so he was winging it. When Ian saw Mick freeze, Ronson said afterwards, 'Well, if you're lost, you might as well stay where you are'. Priceless!

'That Girl Is Rock 'N' Roll'

'That Girl Is Rock 'N' Roll' sounds a bit rougher than the remainder of the LP, which adds life to the effort. This simple, straightforward song is summarised perhaps best by Hunter. The meaning is obvious. Some girls are rock 'n' roll, most aren't. It is obvious when you meet one; it certainly is written from an average male's point of view. We just know.

'Somethin's Goin' On'

The topic of 'Somethin's Goin' On' is serious. It's as if the world were a subway, the human race is an endangered species, and international leaders are muggers. The song expresses the likelihood of a nuclear confrontation and notes a distrust of the political elites. If you sense that war is coming, you notice that something is going on. This song is something like, are you noticing what is going on around you? It is a warning against nuclear war while the leaders can watch from the safety of their planes. Leaders can watch while the people are victims of violence. This is Hunter's cynicism as he reads the papers, and like the average person, they are disgusted by what they see. We are not sure exactly what is going on, but we know something is happening.

'Captain Void 'N' The Video Jets'

Hunter addresses the ridiculousness of television (actually the name of an American show) for a second time, but 'Captain Void 'N' The Video Jets' is in a fanciful and comical mood. This is a bit of an odd tune, but the space visitors concept will be revisited and improved on *Stranded In Reality*. The song is chock full of studio effects and fits in with the remainder of the LP because as a whole, the release is a mixed bag.

'Captain To Candida' starts the song, so it's the captain speaking to yeasts, I suppose, because they spread as fungal infections worldwide. They are machines looking through the glass to hypnotise people. Finally, Hunter states:

We don't hit lovers – we leave them alone
We just hit children who rot in their homes.

The import of the lyrics is the power TV has over people, but here, it is described as an off-the-wall fantasy. The aliens take over through TVs. Hunter speculates he must have been playing a video game and losing when he wrote this. To end with, 'Mr. Jones' the name must stand as an everyman, common name since Mick Jones did not participate in the effort as he had on *Short Back 'N' Sides*.

'Seeing Double'

Some have argued that 'Seeing Double' is the standout track of the album. Hunter's reverie is bolstered by Peter Frampton band member Bob Mayo and Clarence Clemons. The penultimate song of the LP is about a mixed-up sad character that is along the lines of 'All of the Good Ones Are Taken'. It is a live recorded improvisation in the studio. Bob Mayo is the standout on the keyboards for this organic song and Hunter has a soft spot for the tune, seeming like a memory of a hangover. He likes the song and it is the only organic song on the release. It is a sad little song about feeling that you are at the end of your rope.

'All Of The Good Ones Are Taken' (Slow Version)

See above.

Related Songs
'Traitor'

A limited edition *All Of The Good Ones Are Taken* twelve-inch disc was pressed in the UK containing 'Traitor' which is a non-LP track. It was written by Hunter with input from Robbie Alter with an up-tempo call-and-response lyric and fabulous glissando piano from Mandel. The sound effects were reminiscent of *Short Back 'N' Sides* but showed how experimentation can work when done effectively. The track was as strong as anything on the regular release.

The song reminds me of a soundtrack song that would fit Hunter's 1980s output for a movie. In some ways, it is similar to 'Bastard' since it is about love that went wrong. Here is one clever phrase:

You're so shallow, you try to get
Your feet in your mouth but they never get wet

The title from the 1956 hit 'The Girl Can't Help It' recorded by Little Richard, is included in the lyrics as well. It is a manufactured song during a period that Hunter says he was not writing well and it definitely is not about Ronson. Hunter doesn't remember much about it.

Hunter's 80s Hiatus

Critics were mixed and there was limited press about the release, but the LP failed to chart in Britain. In the US, the release spent eleven weeks on the *Billboard* chart. The fast version of the title song, backed by 'Death 'N' Glory Boys', reached number 25 on *Billboard*'s Mainstream Rock Songs chart.

No live dates were scheduled to promote the release and Hunter has mixed feelings about the release in hindsight. There were good songs, but it didn't really make a splash. The label dropped it and made no effort to promote the album.

The musical wilderness following the release resulted in a self-imposed musical retreat for six years, but Hunter was involved in some work and collaborations during this time. For The Payola$, he sang on 'I'll Find Another (Who Can Do It Right)' for the 1983 LP *Hammer On A Drum*. With Blue Öyster Cult's Eric Bloom and Donald Roeser, he co-wrote 'Let Go' and 'Goin' Through The Motions'. For Michael Monroe's Hanoi Rocks, he did the chorus and put together 'Boulevard Of Broken Dreams'. With the band Mountain, Hunter appeared on 'Go For Your Life'.

From 1984-1987 Hunter's compositions were never released as he took time off. Songs were done in his home studio as he avoided the drugs and corporate excesses of the 1980s. In 1985, he got a place on the South Coast, living an ordinary life with kids, near his mates Miller and Fiona Anderson in Shoreham, where the Hunters had an apartment on the Worthing seafront. One of the former inhabitants of the flat was Sir Frederick Adair Roe, head of the Bow Street Runners, eventually the subject of a Hunter song, 'Bow Street Runners'. The retreat allowed Ian to spend time with his youngest son, Jesse, since he had missed the childhood of his first two children.

In 1986, Hunter's son was five, and he was back in the music game by playing a series of dates in Canada and American gigs with the Roy Young Band. Early rocker Young would appear lyrically in the song 'Bed Of Roses'. When Hunter asked, Roy told him how he was offered a spot in the Beatles. Answering how he felt about turning the band down, he said every day when he got out of bed, he banged his head against a wall, but other than that, he was okay. Back in Britain, Young worked with Nicol Williamson, whom Ian had written a song for before he joined Mott. Young introduced him to twenty-one-year-old Pat Kilbride, a prodigious bassist who would later join Hunter's band; and, during this period, he wrote 'The Other Man', a song that would not appear until *Ian Hunter's Dirty Laundry*. As Hunter prepared for his *YUI Orta* release, he toured North American dates in November 1987 with Young and tried out his new material before live audiences. Some of the strong songs that Ian started writing, which kindled Ronson's interest in playing guitar and recording again, included: 'Look Before You Leap', 'Ill Wind', 'The Loner' and '(I'm The) Teacher', Ronson's 'Sweet Dreamer', Little Steven's 'While You Were Looking At Me' and 'American Music'. The trio of Hunter, Ronson, Young and his band toured Ontario in June 1988.

57

'(I'm The) Teacher'

A first-ever movie composition, '(I'm The) Teacher' was a song to order by movie people, but Hunter considers it to contain one of his best lyrics. The movie producer was a fan and Ian had a lyric in mind: 'The question's arisen, is this a prison, some say it is, some say it isn't'. And the rest came quickly. Starting with that first strong line, the remainder of the lyrics came in five minutes. With a good line, you have won half the battle. Ian had the movie script and he read the log line. There was more interaction between Hunter and the producer since originally the song was a ballad but a faster song was required. Revved up with Ronson's help, Ian got a gold record, so not much to complain about!

Hunter does appropriately demonstrate the dedication of many teachers:

If there's just one weed in this flowerless grave
If there's just one seed I can save
I'm going to reach ya
Pleased to meet ya, I'm the teacher

The song appeared in the United Artists 1984 comedy *Teachers* starring Nick Nolte.

'Great Expectations (You Never Know What To Expect)'

This was written for Orion Pictures' college comedy movie *Up The Creek*. Hunter first recorded it with Virgin Records' heavy metal band Shooting Star. In a sense, this song is about Ian's daughter Tracie but more tongue-in-cheek. She is an independent person and Hunter works to stay in her good graces. Ian went to Pasha Music in LA, but the band couldn't play the song correctly, since it seemed simple, but Hunter's music was more sophisticated when actually performed. Displeased with the sound, Ian sent a demo that he created instead and what we hear is the result.

'Good Man In A Bad Time' (Marc Tanner and Jon Reede)

Hunter and Ronson covered 'Good Man In A Bad Time', written by Marc Tanner and Jon Reede. The producer and DJ Arthur Baker asked Hunter to perform the song since he liked his voice. Ian recorded this in Baker's Manhattan Studio for use in the 1985 horror movie *Fright Night*. The song is absolutely ideal for accompanying the visuals in the film. The film follows a young man who discovers that his next-door neighbour is a vampire.

'Wake Up Call' (Baker/Tina B/Mandel)

Another song done for DJ and producer Arthur Baker. The call from Baker was a surprise for Hunter, asking him to do the vocals for the 1986 independently made American action-fantasy sci-fi film *The Wraith* with Charlie Sheen. It only took one day. Overall, Ian worked with Baker for a week and they got along well. A song, 'Professional Lover', was supposed to go to Tina Turner, which sounded like a great idea, but apparently, Arthur did not follow up. In any case, Hunter liked the sound that Baker got and one track for a film was lucrative; by putting energy into one song, you are done in two days.

Other artists recorded Hunter's compositions. Karla DeVito, who worked with Meatloaf, recorded Hunter-Mandel's 'Money Can't Buy Love' for *Wake 'Em Up In Tokyo*. Usually, money can't buy love, except sometimes, but Hunter says it can buy ornamental fringes. In 1987, Scott Folsom recorded Hunter's 'Red Letter Day' and their co-written 'White On White'.

Also in 1987, Ian played piano on four tracks for Michael Monroe's *Nights Are So Long* album, and importantly, he connected with John Jansen, known for the Cutting Crew hit '(I Just) Died In Your Arms', especially assisting on a track called 'Abnormal' for Hunter and 'American Music'.

The association with Jansen proved to be fortuitous since Hunter was back and prepared for his next effort, as the latter song would be recorded for *YUI Orta*.

From the infectious hooks of *All Of The Good Ones Are Taken* to the rocking allure of *YUI Orta*, Hunter embraced a fusion of harder rock and introspective up-tempo rockers. Ian delved deep into the human experience, exploring themes of love, loss, and self-reflection. From the anthemic power of 'American Music' to the soul-stirring beauty of 'Sweet Dreamer', each track reveals a new facet of Hunter's multifaceted artistry.

YUI Orta

Personnel:
Ian Hunter: lead vocals, backing vocals, piano on 'Sweet Dreamer'
Mick Ronson: guitars, backing vocals
Pat Kilbride: bass
Tommy Mandel: keyboards
Mickey Curry: drums
Joe Cerisano: backing vocals
Carmella Long: backing vocals
Donnie Kehr: backing vocals
Robbie Alter: backing vocals
Carola Westerlund: backing vocals
Bernard Edwards: bass on 'Women's Intuition'
Benny Marshall: vocals on bonus tracks
Produced at: Power Station, New York City, Bernard Edwards
Release date: 3 October 1989 UK and 22 January 1990 USA
Running time: 71:11
Current edition: Mercury
Highest chart places: UK: 72, US: 157

Hunter teamed up with the illustrious John Jansen, along with a triumphant reunion of Hunter and his long-time musical compadre, Ronno. The duo embarked on a whirlwind tour, accompanied by long-time rocker Roy Young and his Band. The Slimmer Twins were ready to reclaim their rightful place in the rock pantheon.

Bob Ridge of Variety Artists pushed for the Twins to tour and informally, they were HRB touring between 27 September and 4 December 1988 for sixty shows and considered naming the next record *American Music, Balance* and later *Wish*. The Canadian trio of Shawn Eisenberg on drums, bassist Pat Kilbride, and keyboardist Howard Helm backed the Twins. By early 1989, European dates were scheduled, but drumming duties were completed by the addition of Londoner Steve Holley, who would later figure as one of the most instrumental members of The Rant Band. The core band can be heard on *The Hunter Ronson Band BBC Live In Concert*.

The title of the release was an adaptation of 'Why you, I oughta ... ', a comedy phrase by American wisecrackers The Three Stooges. While beginning the recording, Hunter assisted Mick Jones of Foreigner on 'Just Wanna Hold' and the song was credited to Jones, Hunter, M. Phillips (widely believed to be Mick Jagger since he had warbled a bit on a demo for the track). Ian also played piano, co-produced the track, and appeared in the promo video. For the recording, Holley worked with Joe Cocker, so drummer Mickey Curry substituted while keyboardist Tommy Mandel joined as well.

All songs were written by Ian Hunter except where noted.

'American Music'

Hunter started working with John Jansen in 1987 on 'American Music', which is a majestic tribute to the great early rockers that inspired Ian to pursue music and also features a terrific video montage with Ian and the late great Ronson on guitar. Ronson got interested in playing guitar again and getting back to recording with strong songs such as this one. The video was filmed at a disused mental institution at Teddington in Middlesex, which accompanied the song.

Hunter writes of dreaming to get out of his humdrum youth with 'honky tonk heroes' of American music from Memphis, Harlem, Nashville, New Orleans, and the Windy City. Hunter has noted his fascination with American cities, history and names at times, and this tune is a celebration of American music that crossed the pond and touched him during his youth in England. The celebration of youth and music that inspired Ian is brilliantly portrayed by picturing a young boy playing air guitar in the mirror.

'The Killer', Jerry Lee Lewis, is one of the most highly visible and appropriately depicted stars in the video since he was a big influence on Ian. The blandness of the black-and-white world of Hunter's British upbringing accurately contrasts Ian's youth with the joy of American music. An English kid bearing a resemblance to the floppy blonde-haired locks of Jerry Lee looks longingly at a music store and dreams of what could be.

The pioneers and groundbreaking artists such as Lewis that appear are Muddy Waters, Chuck Berry, Otis Redding (including a direct tribute quoting 'Sitting On The Dock Of The Bay'), Bill Haley, and Little Richard.

This is one of those songs that seems like it should have been a hit since it had so many things going for it. Great guitar work by Ronson, a tribute to the power of rock by Ian, and a strong marketing video push.

Writing the song, Hunter resisted calling it by the title since it sounded like it could be an Exxon commercial, but there was no way around it. After three months, he felt it was complete and continues to be a sincere tribute to American music. As kids, they listened to the Light Program on the BBC, but twice a week, they would play 'Whole Lotta Shakin' Goin On' or 'Hound Dog'. Young people listened all the time since there was no warning when the good music was coming on. Ian says it was like a letter from a friend when the great tunes came across the airwaves.

'The Loner'

'The Loner' is one of his autobiographical songs, which explains some of his lyrics and his music can be understood best when you grasp his background. As a stranger in a strange land, as on 'When I'm President', he informs us of his birthday, horoscope, family life, and youthful environs: all in the first verse! Hunter addresses his early years in Shrewsbury when he had no friends, and he thinks it's one of the best songs he has ever written, reminding him of something that Free would have done in the 1960s. It came quickly one morning and he got it down quick on an acoustic guitar since rockers such as this don't come that often. Ronson's fuzzed-up, slow-burning riff was one of the elements that got him interested in playing guitar again and working with Hunter because of strong songs such as this. Oddly, a big heavy metal band in America asked for a rocker song and Hunter offered this tune, but they never returned the call. The demo with Robbie Alter is a killer, which kicked off the song. Alter is clouded with echo, flashing a bit for his part, and then, with no echo, there is his great solo.

'Women's Intuition' (Hunter/Ronson)

The Slimmer Twins wrote this song together and it was one of the last tracks for the album. It sounds similar to The Rolling Stones, as if they were still performing compelling music. This is a song similar to 'Bastard' in that it sounds realistic and what being in a relationship can be like. The woman is like Judas and is used synonymously with betrayal, as he was the disciple who betrayed Jesus to the Sanhedrin in the Garden of Gethsemane by kissing him on the cheek to reveal his identity for arrest. A woman involved with a musician is always whining, yet: 'I gave you the best years of your miserable life'.

The woman went wrong somewhere but should listen to her woman's intuition, or she will end up on her ass. The song is about Ronson and Hunter writing about women who want to break up a band or keep a musician from the music. Men and women need to work it out: aggression vs. possession. Bernard Edwards played bass.

'Tell It Like It Is' (Hunter/Ronson)

'Tell It Like It Is' is a co-written track with Ronson and echoes the 1960 'Shakin' All Over' hit by Johnny Kidd & The Pirates as an up-tempo rocker. Kidd was one of the few British artists to have worldwide success in the pre-Beatle period. With a paucity of lyrics, the song is held together by rocking musically. It sounds like it has a nod to T-Rex's 'Get It On' which had paid homage to Chuck Berry's 'Little Queenie'. In short, it is a tribute to class rock 'n' roll and rock forebears.

'Livin' In A Heart'

'Livin' In A Heart' was first titled 'Angel' but not the same song as on *Defiance Part 1*. It is a classic Hunter ballad, referencing Ian's marital breakup and visits a similar theme as on 'Waterlow': guilt and regret. This song is about lost love, and maybe the guy is the reason for causing family pain, so he apologises about his lust for success, leading him to neglect his love. Probably more than one pursuer of commercial happiness can relate when they have made a choice to neglect a personal love for the height of fame. It's a gentle, reflective, and thoughtful tune about heredity and genetics. Upon reflection, Ian thinks family is more important than anything else, but he has put music before them at times, which causes grief. This song is an apology for making a mistake years ago; it's about atonement.

How could I turn away love, how could I turn into stone
How could I turn my back on you
I wanted to be a success but success never leaves you alone
Maybe I tried a little too hard
Maybe I pushed you way too far

'Big Time'

When touring in early 1989, this song was called 'You're Never Too Small To Hit The Big Time' until the title was shortened to 'Big Time'. This tune seems like the ultimate road song about how no matter how small you are you can still make it. It is an optimistic piano-based boogie in the style of 'Once Bitten Twice Shy' and it deals with hope. Is it wishful thinking by the untalented or more biographical since Ian didn't seem to enjoy his claim to fame during his most popular era? And, it can be interpreted as in his diary, *Diary Of A Rock N' Roll Star*, that fame is not all it is cracked up to be because your heart grows cold. The road is tedious, unhealthy, and filled with temptation, but 'you are never too small to make the big time'. Artists strive for stardom no matter what the drawbacks are.

Hunter moved back to Manhattan in 1985 to kick-start his writing and this was the first song that emerged. The move immediately reinvigorated his work. He wrote this tune after only two months, which got him thinking he could get a few more for an album. The record is about hope and as a reminder, it should be played during early morning work for motivation. If you are single-minded, you will develop the focus needed to do better. Anything can happen.

'Cool' (Hunter/Ronson)

With 'Cool', Ian teamed up with his old mate Ronson once again to write and record this song and album in the middle of 1989. Ian and Mick had toured the USA and Europe in late 1988-early 1989, before the album was even recorded, and the result is a highly polished album and one of their best. The team was tight and the LP demonstrated their exemplary collaboration.

Originally, the song was entitled 'Cool Jerk', and Hunter is identifying the herd mentality of people who won't change their minds. The song is a cloying look at the idea of being 'cool' or a hipster since every society has some people within that group who decide these things. As Ian identifies the cool people, he points out that it can be anyone highly placed or an ordinary everyday person; the point of the song is to oppose the cool people because the singer says:

But don't you ever cross me dude
'Cos that ain't cool, that's an attitude

The song features kicking drum beats, wah-wah guitar and synthesized brass, the punchy song noting all trendy things.

'Beg A Little Love' (Hunter/McNasty)
Some thought 'Beg A Little Love' was the strongest track on the effort and is co-written by Hunter and R. McNasty, a pseudonym for guitarist Robbie Alter. This is a dramatic and personal tune with galloping drum patterns and twisting Ronson guitar contributions. The song is a profound statement of growing, coming of age, and learning in life. When the harshest experiences in life come at you so you look for that perfect stranger and you beg a little love; even at the end of the song, he inverts age with the closing lines, 'I'm still a child/And I get down on my knees and I beg/Beg a little love', brilliant! Hunter has numerous religious allusions even in the most secular of contexts and this one is no different with a 'sacrificial lamb' along with a bit of echoing his Mott The Hoople song 'When My Mind's Gone' reprised with:

When my mind had gone, when both o' my minds had gone
When my minds had gone.

No matter what our age, we seem to always want the same things and Hunter says this is a song to himself. The lyrics are among his favourites as the best on the record and a diary of someone floundering in middle life.

'Following In Your Footsteps' (Hunter/Ronson)
This one is about heredity, genetics, and not wanting to be like your father. Two key lines are:

You never got what you wanted
So I never got what I need

If the father is deficient, then the child will not get what they need. The child has to follow in the footsteps of what they know. The 'someone' is the father knowing that:

Someone must have given me anger,
someone must have given me hate
Or why would I stand here shakin',
when there's so many chances to take

With all these drawbacks, the child is inhibited when there are so many things to do and possibilities in life. The genes can hold you back. The frustration that Hunter had with his father is explored in 'Ships' and 'No Hard Feelings'. Ian realises that his father had a really difficult life with war and the Great Depression. Then, his father got stuck in a job as a cop. Hunter

Left: In March 1975, Hunter joined forces with Mick Ronson. Hunter's first single from his eponymous solo album was the UK Top 40 hit 'OBT'. (*Circus Raves*)

Right: Hunter's first studio album of the 1980s was *Short Back 'N' Sides* (1981), produced in collaboration with Ronson and Clash guitarist Mick Jones. (*Ray Palmer*)

Left: The Apex Skiffle Group, with Hunter on the far right. Hunter's first gigs were at the Old White Hart in Northampton. His early days in Northampton form the subject of 'Rain'. (*Derrick A. Thompson & William Martin*)

Right: 'I don't even have one of these', Hunter stated as he signed this 'And I Have Learned To Dream' 7" single – his first songwriting credit from 1967 – at a gig on 2 July 2013. (From the collection of *The Doctor of Digital™ G. Mick Smith, PhD*)

Left: This issue of *L.A.'s Phonograph Record Magazine* was autographed after the gig at the City Winery, NYC on 25 June 2016. (From the collection of *The Doctor of Digital™ G. Mick Smith, PhD*)

Right: A Hollywood Palladium advert for a Mott The Hoople gig on 14 September 1973. I caught a ride to Hollywood to see my first-ever rock concert featuring Mott The Hoople. (*G. Mick Smith, PhD*)

Left: A swimming Hunter captured on camera! Former MTH bandmate Morgan Fisher sent these pictures directly to me, signed: 'To Mick from Morgan Fisher'. (*Screenshots from Morgan Fisher's DVD Mott In America*)

Right: To supplement the 1973 American tour, Mick Bolton and Morgan Fisher were added on keyboards. The picture is signed: 'To Mick from Malvern!!! Morgan Fisher'. (*Screenshots from Morgan Fisher's DVD Mott In America*)

Left: Hunter's self-titled debut album introduced the world to music with a burning desire to break free from the shackles of pop conformity. (*CBS*)

Right: *All American Alien Boy* was commercial suicide, but thematically, it anticipates much of Hunter's later first-rate work, revisited during the remainder of his career. (*Columbia*)

Left: On the ill-fated *Overnight Angels* release, Ian is depicted with his signature sunglasses and corkscrew hair. (*Columbia*)

Right: Reunited with Ronson, Hunter crafted one of his finest albums, *You're Never Alone With A Schizophrenic*, a best-selling effort after two poorly-selling albums. (*Chrysalis*)

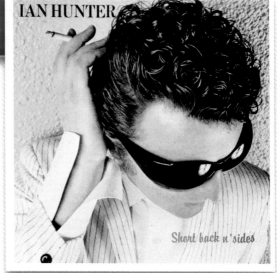

Left: *Welcome To The Club* served a dual purpose: it captured Hunter's electrifying performances whilst also weaving in a handful of tantalising studio gems. (*Chrysalis*)

Right: In 1981, *Short Back 'N' Sides* was a curious offering, leaving fans divided and intrigued in equal measure. (*Chrysalis*)

Left: In this 24-30 April 1975 issue of Scene magazine, Hunter stated: 'I see all these screaming birds all over the stage, and, of course, it's for Ronno'. (From the collection of *The Doctor of Digital™ G. Mick Smith, PhD*)

Right: Interviewed about *All American Alien Boy* by Jim Girard in *Scene* magazine, Ian stated: 'Even when it didn't look like I was into taste, I was'. (From the collection of *The Doctor of Digital™ G. Mick Smith, PhD*)

Above: The Capitol Theatre (now demolished) triptych promo for the Ian Hunter Band showing a local record store Disc-O-Mat advert for *All American Alien Boy* and flyer for 21 October 1979. (*The Doctor of Digital™ G. Mick Smith, PhD*)

Right: The well-known Agora gig on 18 June 1979 was part of the extensive American tour promoting the successful *You're Never Alone With A Schizophrenic* album. (From the collection of *The Doctor of Digital™ G. Mick Smith, PhD*)

Left: Hunter appeared at the Licorice Pizza record store on 31 May 1980, marking the occasion by autographing my poster. Ian also signed my inside gatefold of the first Mott LP. (From the collection of *The Doctor of Digital™ G. Mick Smith, PhD*)

Right: The Creem Stars Cars featured Ian twice, and circa 1983, Ian loaned this car out to bassist Mark Clarke for a couple of days. (*Lynn Goldsmith*)

Left: From the Veterans Memorial gig on 21 September 1979, Ian, Mick and George Meyer are pictured here on the longest tour Hunter has ever been on. (*The Doctor of Digital*™ *G. Mick Smith, PhD*)

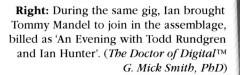

Right: During the same gig, Ian brought Tommy Mandel to join in the assemblage, billed as 'An Evening with Todd Rundgren and Ian Hunter'. (*The Doctor of Digital*™ *G. Mick Smith, PhD*)

Left: Todd Rundgren and Ian Hunter performing at The Agora, Cleveland, OH on 19 October 1980. Generally non-political, Ian played 12 charity concerts with Todd in support of Congressman John Anderson, an independent candidate in the 1980 US presidential election. (*The Doctor of Digital*™ *G. Mick Smith, PhD*)

Left: Ian pointing while the group play several of Ian's songs and covers. (*The Doctor of Digital*™ *G. Mick Smith, PhD*)

Above: Ian also gigged with Todd for a benefit for Vietnam Vets. (*The Doctor of Digital*™ *G. Mick Smith, PhD*)

Left: Ronson joined for the Cleveland concert, but prior to the Dr. Pepper concert in New York, Mick announced he was leaving the collaboration. (*The Doctor of Digital*™ *G. Mick Smith, PhD*)

Ian Hunter

Left: *All Of The Good Ones Are Taken* had everything going for it: strong songs, a terrific band, clever marketing and solid 1980s rock. (*Columbia*)

All of The Good Ones Ar...

Right: Hunter and Ronson, as The Slimmer Twins, teamed up with producer John Jansen and toured with long-time rocker Roy Young and his Band to promote *YUI Orta*. (*Mercury*)

Left: The tragedy of Ronson's passing would soon befall the rock world, but the *BBC Live In Concert* live album permanently blazes. (*Windsong Records*)

Right: For *Dirty Laundry,* the rogue-like Casino Steel and the visionary Bjørn Nessjø conceived a project like no other: The Gringo Starrs. (*Cherry Red*)

Left: Finding his footing again after Ronson's passing, Hunter began his exceptional later career with Bjørn Nessjø on *Artful Dodger.* (*Citadel*)

Right: Beginning with *Rant*, the core of The Rant Band – drummer Steve Holley, guitarist James Mastro, and guitarist and producer extraordinaire Andy York – energise the string of later first-rate releases. (*Papillion*)

Left: The audacious *Strings Attached* – with strings and Hunter's moniker of 'Sigmund and the Little Freuds' – was pulled off with Bjørn Nessjø and Andy York. (*Proper Records*)

Right: With almost the same set list as *Strings Attached*, *The Truth, The Whole Truth, And Nuthin' But The Truth* demonstrates how Ian never looks back and features appearances by Mick Ralphs, Joe Elliott and Brian May. (*Secret Records*)

Left: A counterpoint to the English-based *Rant*, *Shrunken Heads* sets its sights on the USA and short attention spans, endless texting and painfully stilted conversations. (*Jerkin Crocus*)

Right: The Ranters coalesced for *Man Overboard*, the taping, overdubbing and mixing of which took only two weeks. (*New West Records*)

Left: Hunter tackles social and political issues with wit and swagger on *When I'm President*. It is worth noting that this release is the first of three consecutive studio albums on the charts since 1989. (*Proper Records*)

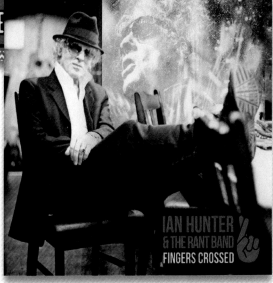

Right: Hunter addresses the themes of love, resilience and the indomitable spirit of rock on *Fingers Crossed* – the recordings took only four days! (*Proper Records*)

Left: A red *YUI Orta* advert, with tour dates listed at the bottom, from 3 October 1989. (From the collection of *The Doctor of Digital™ G. Mick Smith, PhD*)

Right: An advert for the 20 May 2000 London Astoria show. The concert was part of Hunter's UK tour and was recorded and released as a live album titled *Just Another Night: Live At The Astoria, London.* (From the collection of *The Doctor of Digital™ G. Mick Smith, PhD*)

Left: A poster for the 2 December 2012 show at The Paramount, Huntington, NY. At this show, Hunter promoted his latest album *When I'm President* and Graham Parker reunited with The Rumour for *Three Chords Good*, celebrating over 30 years of music. (From the collection of *The Doctor of Digital™ G. Mick Smith, PhD*)

Right: A shot of Ian at the 18 November 2011 show at The Havana, New Hope, PA. If you get up close at a gig, you might notice the Roland piano's transformation into 'Ian' with the help of some black tape. (*The Doctor of Digital*™ *G. Mick Smith, PhD*)

Left: The Ranters at the 30 November 2014 gig at Infinity Hall, Norfolk, CT. From left to right: Dennis Debrizzi, Mark Bosch, Ian, Steve Holley, James Mastro and Paul Page. (*The Doctor of Digital*™ *G. Mick Smith, PhD*)

Right: Ian & The Rant Band headlined the 10th Annual Pleasantville Music Festival on 12 July 2014. I attended three nights in a row on both Coasts, six times in a month. (*The Doctor of Digital*™ *G. Mick Smith, PhD*)

Left: The Ranters rock on *Live In The UK 2010*, with Ian's comment on ATYD: 'I'm lusting for you and at my age that's quite an achievement'. (*Rant Records*)

Right: The expansive *Stranded In Reality* box set is a time capsule of Hunter's solo career, with rare and unreleased treasures waiting to be rediscovered. (*Proper Records*)

Left: There should be no doubt now that Ian is entitled to the Lifetime Achievement award for assembling a stellar cast for *Defiance Part 1*. (*Sun Records*)

reconciled with his father, but the song relates how important he was as he was growing up in his father's footsteps and how fatherhood is critical.

'Sons 'N' Lovers'

'Sons 'N' Lovers' is an autobiographical song and is a companion piece to 'Sons And Daughters', but more focused on his former wife initially, but then the perspective shifts to represent the hurt experienced by the son. It's a sad song about the end of a relationship with his wife and how his son was hurt as well. Hunter's son was eight years old at the time and it is his thoughts about his son's relationship with his mother. Kids have strong feelings and jealousies and cling to their mothers, but they know the damage experienced when a father leaves. The mother is left behind and it hurts. It is an odd subject, but Hunter never seems to shy away from difficult or emotional topics.

'Pain' (Hunter/Kehr)

Ronson and Ian produced this forceful record 'Pain' for Urgent, *Cast The First Stone*, which reached *Billboard*'s Top 100 and sold over 400,000 copies with Donnie Kehr. Kehr gets a co-writing credit on this song, and this song arose out of their collaboration. The song came from that album and Kehr, although a good singer appearing on two Grammy Award-winning albums, went on to be a successful actor as well. Originally entitled 'Pain (Love Is a Victim)', the song featured Tommy Mandel on keyboards. Ronson added a great deal with his muscular guitar work with powerful chords and delightful choruses. Mick's spikey solo was riddled with controlled feedback and superbly performed. The song is about lost love and the pain that results. It says it's going to take some time to get over the suffering. On the Hunter Ronson version, Tommy Mandel played a terrific piano piece with feedback from Mick.

Hunter wrote a total of four songs for Donnie Kehr and the 'Running Back' single hit number 87 on *Billboard*. Ian also co-wrote 'If This Is Love' and 'Inch By Inch'.

'How Much More Can I Take'

The snappy tune 'How Much More Can I Take' is Beatles-esque and with Hunter's relationship lyrics resulting in the Hunter-Ronson teamwork in full-tilt rocking mode. It's a powerful statement of waiting and wondering and most of us have been there at one time or another. It's the emptiness that you feel while waiting for love. The lyrics end with a rhetorical and emotional outpouring:

You fill my eyes
But you don't fill the hunger
How much more can I take

65

Hunter doesn't remember much about it other than he thinks it's too fast. Most of us can relate to the sentiment, though, when we wonder how much worse things can get. The protagonist is unable to tolerate love, rejects it, and then yearns for the unattainable, and in some ways, the track is somewhat reminiscent of 'Arms And Legs'.

'Sweet Dreamer' (Gibson/Ronson)

This song arose from an interpretation of country music superstar Don Gibson's 'Sweet Dreams', whose most famous version of the tune was by Patsy Cline. Hunter and Ronson listened to the song on the road tour bus and then, as adapted by the creative mind of Ronson, the song became an instrumental and was also a part of live shows with a version available from 1989.

Mick loved slow and simple songs and he made it his own and something really special. Hunter says this is his all-time favourite Ronno solo. This was Mick as a master of style applying electric lead guitar to a country standard. Hunter added a bit of gospel piano.

The bonus tracks on the 2003 CD re-release do not include Hunter but consist of tracks related to Mick Ronson.

Conclusion

Critics generally praised *YUI Orta*. The album hit 157 on *Billboard* but did not chart in Britain. It was marketed by Mercury Records with the 'American Music' single and 'Women's Intuition'.

The band played twenty-five concerts during January and February 1990 and crowds celebrated, but some members of the press flaunted ageism. It was poor timing that Ian's mother, Freda Patterson, had passed away in early 1989 and unfortunately, he was aware of bad reviews.

Poor sales scuttled further discussion of additional touring or label interest in another recording. Label upheaval ended any further promotion, which killed the record. Hunter reflects that perhaps the production is lacking but was still proud of 'Following In Your Footsteps' and 'Sweet Dreamer'.

Respectfully disagreeing with Hunter, this was the most powerful and hardest-rocking album of his solo career, but once again, his career appeared to be at a standstill despite producing an exceptionally strong effort.

If that were not bad enough, a horrible tragedy was about to strike.

The rock scene was abuzz with the release of Hunter's *YUI Orta* and the songs came alive as Hunter joined forces with guitar virtuoso Ronson to form The Hunter Ronson Band. Their musical chemistry and boundless energy are beautifully captured in *BBC Live In Concert*. The show consisted of old Hunter favorites like the UK Top Ten hit by his old group Mott the Hoople, 'All The Way From Memphis', and his own UK Top 40 hit 'Once Bitten Twice Shy', plus six songs from the album, including powerful Hunter compositions like 'Following In Your Footsteps' and 'Big Time'.

The Hunter Ronson Band BBC Live In Concert

Personnel
Ian Hunter: vocals, guitar
Mick Ronson: guitar, backing vocals
Pat Kilbride: bass
Howard Helm: keyboards
Drums: Steve Holley
Engineer: Dave Mulkeen
Producer: Pete Ritzema
Produced at: Windsong Records
Release date: 8 October 1995
Running time: 79:34
Current edition: Roir Imports
Highest chart places: Did not chart

A tragedy would soon befall the rock world, but this album crackles with raw energy as Hunter teams up with legendary guitarist Ronson, delivering a powerhouse performance that sets the stage ablaze.

One critical addition to Hunter's bandmates was marked by the arrival of Steve Holley on drums, who will be an important component of Ian's musical efforts and the first step in the forthcoming Rant Band.

'(Give Me Back My) Wings' (Hunter)

Hunter began working with John Jansen in 1987, but '(Give Me Back My) Wings' is a song that fell through the cracks; it was demoed and was the first song proposed for *YUI Orta,* but it didn't make the cut; it was released live in 1989. The theme is mysterious and as lofty as the existence of God as in the song 'God (Take 1)'. Here, in order to have wings, Hunter says:

First it was the Mothers
Then it was the wives
I think that God's a woman
I know she runs my life
And she can still
Oh and I wonder when

It is a reflective track and Hunter is considering how much he owes his family. The persona of Ian Hunter rock star results in drama at times, but this is an acknowledgement of how much he owes others and a higher power.

Robbie Alter lived next to Ian in NYC and put an amazing sound down on guitar. Originally, it was a ballad with Alter, but David Letterman's drummer, Anton Figg, came to Hunter's house in Katonah and rearranged the song. Producer Bernard Edwards nixed it for *YUI Orta* because it didn't equate with balancing the entire release. Live, the song was done with Ronson on

67

his Telecaster, and since Hunter rarely looks back, the song was just dropped from a regular release, but he liked it. The live song was a showcase for the young Pat Kilbride, who just kicks on this track.

Now, we navigate the bittersweet journey from the electrifying experience of The Hunter Ronson Band to the heartbreaking loss that befell the music world with the tragic passing of the legendary Mick Ronson. Yet, from the depths of sorrow emerged the resilience of Ian Hunter as he paved his own path with *Dirty Laundry*.

Ian Hunter's Dirty Laundry

Personnel:
Ian Hunter: guitars, vocals
Casino Steel (Stein Groven): keyboards, vocals, percussion
'Honest' John Plain (John Splain): guitar, vocals
Darrell Bath: guitar, vocals
Glen Matlock: bass
Steve 'Vom' Ritchie: drums
Blue Weaver: keyboards
Lasse Hafreager: piano, organ
Mitt Gamon: harmonica
Angela Clemmons-Patrick, Bård Svendsen, James Williams, Torstein Flakne,
Vaneese Thomas: backing vocals
Torstein Flakne: guitar on 'Invisible Strings'
Produced at Abbey Road Studios. Final vocals recorded at Nidaros Studio,
Trondheim, Norway by Bjørn Nessjø
Release date: 10 October 1995
Running time: 49:59
Current edition: Cherry Red
Highest chart places: Did not chart

Ian Hunter leads us through a captivating studio transition from the thematic
depths of *YUI Orta* to the raw and gritty brilliance of *Dirty Laundry*. From
the electrifying riffs of 'Another Fine Mess' to the haunting introspection of
'Red Letter Day', each track unveils a new layer of Hunter's artistic evolution.
Collaborating with a stellar line-up of artful dodgers, he infuses his music
with infectious energy, blistering guitar solos, and his signature growl.

The tale of the release intertwines tragedy, friendship, and a whirlwind
of musical creativity. It all started when the rogue-like Casino Steel and the
visionary Bjørn Nessjø conceived a project like no other: The Gringo Starrs.
Their quest for sonic brilliance led them to the indomitable Hunter.

But before destiny fully unfolded its hand, Hunter and his faithful companion
Ronson ventured into the Swedish music scene, leaving their mark as Klubb
Rock and the legendary Park Rock during the heady years of 1990-1991.

Fate, it seems, had a different plan in store. In a twist of cruel irony, Ronson
was struck by the insidious presence of carcinoma of the liver. While Mick's
spirit burned bright, his body faltered. Undeterred by adversity, Hunter
carried on, embarking on a Scandinavian summer tour alongside The Mats
Ronander Band and the spirited Swedish covers group, The Few. Alas, the
music world mourned the loss of Ronson on that fateful day, 29 April 1993.
Yet, in the face of tragedy, Hunter found solace in his art and a renewed drive
to create.

With a newfound urgency, he joined forces with the talented Robbie Alter,
crafting soul-stirring demos that would become the cornerstone of a project

that would soon be known as *Ian Hunter's Dirty Laundry*. In a mere eleven days, they captured the essence of raw rock and roll, channelling the spirit of proto-punk and harkening back to the golden era of The Rolling Stones in 1962. Get ready to dive head-first into a musical odyssey like no other as Hunter lays bare his soul through twelve electrifying tracks. From sorrow to triumph, from tragedy to defiance, this is the tale of *Dirty Laundry*, where the power of music becomes a balm for the wounds of tragedy.

Hunter picked up gigs from time to time. In August 1993, He performed in Europe with Johan Wahlstrom and Ricky Byrd on the Hamn Rock (Harbour Rock) tour. Ian and Byrd appeared as guests of The Mats Ronander Band, in particular at Stockholm's Melody Club, where Hunter first played a new song as a tribute to Ronson entitled 'Michael Picasso'. In September, Hunter appeared on Joe Elliott's *Retroactive* featuring Ian as 'Honky Tonk Messiah' on piano and Ian vocalised the introduction to 'The Golden Age Of Rock 'N' Roll' on their covers album, *Yeah!*

On 29 April 1994, the Mick Ronson Memorial Concert was staged, including a tribute to Mick Ronson and another new song debuted 'Resurrection Mary'.

Seven of the twelve songs were penned or co-written by Hunter. This was the most written by Ian in the studio, which was not his usual modus operandi. Previously and mostly afterwards, he had difficulty writing in the studio. 'Big Kid' was one song that didn't make the cut.

'Dancing On The Moon' (Hunter/Bath/Plain)

'Dancing On The Moon' has a strong live feel to it and it opens the record to a rocking start. The band didn't know what they were doing and the drums were all over the place since Ian kept changing the chords. It is totally spontaneous. Nonetheless, a great feature of the track is a strong chorus filled with some wordplay about being out and about. It feels like the musicians are just giving it all and having a great time letting it all hang out. It reminds me of the sort of creative chaos that Guy Stevens tried to inspire in the *Brain Capers*-era Mott The Hoople. Chaotic but somehow less than polished rock efforts work.

'Another Fine Mess' (Hunter/Bath/Plain)

'Another Fine Mess' can almost apply to the album it appears in, but the project turned out to be stimulating. This song can be viewed as a reflection on life on the road with Ronson: Hunter is Stan Laurel with Ollie Ronson. The title referenced the well-known comedic catchphrase of Laurel and Hardy, the British-American comedy duo during the classic Hollywood era of American cinema.

'Scars' (Hunter/Bath/Plain)

'Scars' is a collaborative effort and a standout, although it was quickly recorded in about an hour while Darrel Bath and Hunter wrote three or four songs in one day. It's a song about a painful break-up. The entire record was done quickly, although Ian felt this song and 'Never Trust A Blonde' were the standout tracks. There are beautiful keyboard touches by Blue Weaver, who toured with Mott The Hoople on their 1973 US tour.

'Never Trust A Blonde' (Bath)
In this collaborative effort, 'Never Trust A Blonde' is Darrel Bath's fun tune after he had been in the Crybabys. The Crybabys from London, UK, were formed by Darrell Bath and Honest John Plain in 1990, but the band broke up when Darrell joined Dogs D'amour in November 1992. Throughout the 90s, Darrell and Honest John recorded several albums credited to the Crybabys, but most of them were never released at the time. Apparently, every blonde is suspect, as the boy in the song was told:

My daddy said, 'Rocky, don't even trust your mom!'

'Psycho Girl' (Plain)
In a similar humorous way as with 'Never Trust A Blonde', 'Psycho Girl' was the contribution by Bath's bandmate in the Crybabys, Honest John Plain. He says:

She's my cross to bear, my ball and chain
A monkey on my back, she gets into my brain
But I love my washed out, freaked out Psycho Girl
Yeah, if I'd known then what I know now
I wouldn't change a thing, no way no how
'Cause I love my blown out, zonked out Psycho Girl

'My Revolution' (Steel/Dangerfield/Hunter)
'My Revolution' is a co-written track, reflecting back on Ian's Mott The Hoople period and was mostly Casino Steel's idea. There is a reference to 'a revolution for fun' arising from the *Mott* LP. Steel liked Mott The Hoople a great deal. The lyrics are about those raucous romps, which included trying to guess whose kid is whose, and the revolution is not for politics but for being randy and partying. That the party can continue in advancing years is noted by the line 'you'd better lock up your mum!'

'Good Girls' (Plain)
During this motley collaboration, Plain also contributed this song and released it by Cleveland International in 1990. The song reached one on the Canadian Singles Chart and 19 on the US *Billboard* Hot 100 in 1990. It also charted in the UK, Australia, and New Zealand. In addition, a music video was released in 1990 and features Honest John Plain performing the song in and around Cleveland, Ohio.

71

'Red Letter Day'

Hunter started working with John Jansen in 1987 on *YUI Orta,* but 'Red Letter Day' didn't get recorded until this effort and it is one of the few solo-written songs on the CD. Here, Hunter is close to his beloved, but one of the difficulties of relationships is that we often cannot see eye to eye with our lovers. We miss each other. The lovers are separated, but once the partners come home together again, it will be alright. The title of the song comes from the idea of any day with special significance and is a phrase rooted in classical antiquity, e.g., important days are indicated in red in Roman Republic calendars. Would it be a surprise that Ian's wife Trudi thinks of it as one of her favourites? It's true.

'Invisible Strings'

'Invisible Strings' is part of the *Dirty Laundry* output but was solely composed by Ian despite the generally collaborative nature of the project. The release is strong enough to appear on a regular Hunter album, but it has not and as such, this is one of the most intriguing of the songs on the collection where the group nature of the project worked.

The song is about the hold that a girl can have in dreams. The invisible strings are the metaphor for how much control that girls can have. At the end, or 'when the fat lady sings', that girl will still have the tie of invisible strings and the guy can't shake her. Hunter thought the song was strong but too wordy to perform live, but reflects a genuine conversation. Perhaps a shame, no?

'Everyone's A Fool' (Bath/Roig)

The 1990s song was mainly written while Roig's role remains unclear. What is clear is that the lyrics indicate a blues-influenced rock sound while the alleyway setting, midnight rendezvous, and themes of infidelity hint at a gritty, atmospheric vibe. The catchy chorus, with its 'fool' and 'wild' repetitions, adds a playful but slightly cynical edge to the narrative.

The song portrays complex relationship dynamics, where the protagonist seeks to justify their ulterior motives while acknowledging the universal human tendencies of deception and lust.

'Junkee Love' (Matheson/Steel)

Hunter played on 'Everyone's A Fool' and 'Junkee Love' but did not write these songs.

The chief songwriter, Casino Steel, had been in the influential Hollywood Brats, who formed in London in 1972 around the songwriting partnership of Steel and, as with this song, Andrew Matheson. Similar in style and looks to The New York Dolls, they were born out of disgust and aimed to shock. The lyrics abound with a darkly romantic theme. The repeated references to needles, syringes, and 'magic misery' paint a picture of addiction and its destructive power within a toxic relationship. The features of stark contrasts ('give me magic misery/first one is free'), vivid imagery ('jump for the juice'), and repetition ('junkee see - junkee do') create a sense of desperation and obsessive dependence. The personification of addiction as a 'poison' and a 'pusher' adds an extra layer of depth and emotional impact.

'The Other Man'
Hunter's time off until 1986 had him composing 'The Other Man', a song that would not appear until *Ian Hunter's Dirty Laundry*. It has an interesting backstory as well. Allegedly, it is from an Everly Brothers recording and Willie Nelson supposedly recorded the song twice, but Ian's manager, Sam Lederman, said none of the recordings ever came to light. As a result, it went on this CD.

The song that ends the CD offers a different perspective from a scorned lover. Usually, the anger is directed towards the woman, but here, the object of disdain is the other man. He forgives the woman for all her misdeeds, but he will never forgive that she may be thinking of that other man.

Conclusion
The final title of the release came as a result of the record label request. The album was issued by Norsk Plateproduksjon in March 1995. The Norwegian label released a promo disc of 'Red Letter Day', then 'My Revolution' was issued as the album's single. The band promoted the song with a live television performance in Oslo on NRK TV's entertainment show *Rondo*. Cleveland International issued the album in America and 'Good Girls' scored highly on several US radio charts.

Not surprisingly, the collaborative release received low-key press coverage but it did gather positive appraisal. The release is one of the significant shifts that Hunter has made during his career, provided an outlet for his music again after a long break, and most importantly, made a creative return following the tragic passing of Ronson.

Ian Hunter takes us on a captivating transition from the gritty and rebellious world of *Dirty Laundry* to the enchanting and introspective realm of *The Artful Dodger*. From the infectious tale of 'Resurrection Mary' to the fanciful musings of 'Skeletons (In Your Closet)', Hunter collaborated with a cadre of exceptional musicians. Ian invited us to run it up and down the flagpole in the sportin' life during the enchanting world of *The Artful Dodger*.

The Artful Dodger

Personnel:
Ian Hunter: lead vocals, acoustic and electric guitars, harp
Darrell Bath: acoustic, electric and Baritone guitars, lead vocals
Torstein Flakne: guitars, vocals
Per Lindvall: drums, percussion
Sven Lindvall: bass
Robbie Alter: acoustic, electric and slide guitars
Kjetil Bjerkestrand: keyboards
Dennis Eliott: drums
Pat Kilbride: bass, acoustic bass
'Honest' John Plain: vocals, lead vocals
Frode Alnaes: guitar
Mariann Lisland: vocals
Per Öisten Sörensen: vocals
The Vertigo String Quartet: strings
Produced at: Nidaros Studios, Trondheim, Norway. Additional recordings at The
Time Machine, Vermont, USA. Michael Picasso recorded live on 4 October 1995,
overdubbed later by Björn Nessjö.
Release date: 1996 (Norway), 21 April 1997 (UK)
Running time: 55:09
Current edition: Citadel
Highest chart places: Did not chart

This new solo album engaged the extraordinary Bjørn Nessjø, a musical
arranger of unparalleled talent. The album's title evolved, starting as
'Life, Get One', thereafter 'Pilgrim's Progress', until finally settling on the
evocative *The Artful Dodger*. Hunter assembled a formidable line-up of
guitarists to fill the void left by the legendary Ronno: Darrell Bath, Robbie
Alter, Frode Alnaes, and Torstein Flakne. The guitarists were joined by
drummer Per Lindvall, keyboardist Kjetil Bjerkestrand, and bassist Sven
Lindvall.

Hunter was on his way back musically by addressing his parents, youth,
NYC, the yellow press, the after-life (possibly), and religion. As with 'Old
Records Never Die', he acknowledged those who passed on with 'Michael
Picasso', 'Walk On Water', and 'Now Is The Time'. Surprisingly, he started the
record off on a low-key note, whereas he usually began with a barn burner.

The verse on the liner notes is pure Darrell Bath. Hunter heard him say
it once and asked him to repeat it, which he did verbatim and Ian wrote it
down. Bath is all rocker and quite the character inspiration for the title of
the album.

'The Artful Dodger' and 'Skeletons (In Your Closet)' attached to this studio
release from the back end of Hunter's previous effort and are a bit out of
place, but similar to songs a bit ill-fitting on Dylan's *Oh Mercy* album. A

74

record is a success if an album hangs together as one piece and since you go in with good intentions, it doesn't always happen, but that's the goal. All songs were written by Hunter unless otherwise noted.

'Too Much'
'Too Much' is an unusual song to open a Hunter CD since it is a slow start, but this is the introduction to the rockers that will follow on the remainder of the release; although, the CD is not as much of a rocker as *Ian Hunter's Dirty Laundry*. Nonetheless, Hunter likes this song a great deal since it is atmospheric with a terrific mood. It is too slow to play live, or Ian would play this favourite.

Hunter is asking if it is too much to be in love. He feels that it may be asking too much and he might not get the answer he would like. He finishes the song with a flourish:

Maybe you don't want me
I'm so scared of losing you
I never miss an opportunity to miss an opportunity
Watch me screw up this one too
It's so hard to talk about love
I'm leaving now, oh it's just
'n all I ever wanted
Was you – is that too much?

'Now Is The Time'
'Now Is The Time' marked a period when Ian got serious about writing again, and producer Bjørn Nessjø was key to this development. After the slack 1980s period, Ian considers this as his first decent song. Hunter started playing it during the summer of 1991 with The Mats Ronander Band and the Swedish covers band The Few; it was especially ready after the 1992 Freddie Mercury Tribute Concert.

Hunter has been known to be able to write personal, heartfelt songs about musical figures he has been associated with and this one is about Freddie Mercury from Queen. There is a clever line revealing the subject as 'that crazy little planet', i.e. Mercury, 'he was a friend of mine'.

Ian and Freddie had a strong professional relationship and Hunter was impressed with him as one of the nicest real stars that he had met. The Freddie Ian knew was always outrageous, real, nice, and as crazy as a loon: the archetypal rock star. Hunter thought of Queen as 'lovely blokes' going back to the early days of Mott when they were on the same bill.

In March 2013, Ian played European and UK live dates as The Ian Hunter Acoustic Trio, with guitarist Andy York and Nashville bassist Dave Roe. The song was recast to target the National Rifle Association instead of referring to Mercury.

'Something To Believe In'

'Something To Believe In' is a song that takes on one of the biggest topics of life: God and faith. The song is related to another look at the topic, 'God (Take 1)' or even 'Salvation'. In short, Hunter is saying that we all need something to believe in. He takes responsibility for hurting others, but he has looked for something to believe in or something more solid. He is not attracted to institutional religion. Nonetheless, we still need something more. Ian broadens his view of international affairs as he refers to Sarajevo and the theme of warfare.

The reference to 'Willy And The Poor Boys' could be a reference to the archetypical American band Creedence Clearwater Revival since that is the title of their fourth album in 1969 and they are lost in America. They might have expressed the sentiment as stranded in 'Lodi', one of their well-known songs. Hunter quotes part of 'laying down to sleep' as a well-known children's bedtime prayer from the 18th Century married to the title, *From Here To Eternity*, a 1953 American drama romance war film, as part of finding something that you can believe in. A really strong verse states his case:

For every seed of knowledge found
For every grain of reason
For every shred of decency
There's something to believe in

It was often performed live, has many verses, and is difficult to learn, but worth it.

'Resurrection Mary' (Hunter/McNasty)

'Resurrection Mary' is a story song about a well-known Chicago area legend. The legend relates that an apparition appears to drivers and there are allusions to the corruption, Mafia, and cronies that are endemic to Chicago, such as Big Jim Colosimo. In a religious experience, the driver hopes to repent and be reborn and then Mary speaks in tongues, which is known as glossolalia. The lyrics evolved over the years between the studio and live versions.

Hunter advises that the song came from seeing a documentary about the legend on *60 Minutes*. Mary is the elusive spectral 'incandescent glow' in the song who was run over by a hit-and-run driver and was never found. The incident occurred on Archer Avenue, and Mary allegedly hitched taxis outside Resurrection Cemetery in Justice, Illinois. The truthful aspect of the song was confirmed by Ian, who called the cemetery to verify that Mary is actually buried there; there is dispute about the specific identification of the Mary in question, though. Hunter is told that this is one of the best songs he'd ever written – and he agrees.

76

'Walk On Water' (Hunter/McNasty)

Hunter co-wrote 'Walk On Water' with Robbie Alter as an oblique narrative along the cryptic style of 'Shallow Crystals' and 'Silver Needles'. The Caledonian swing of the introduction gives sway to a heavy drum beat and sparkling guitar while a tormented soul gets lost in rock 'n' roll and does not come out alive. Ian echoes the spirit of Guy Stevens in this song and could refer to Kurt Cobain, who died in April 1994; Hunter has not identified a specific individual.

Pushed too far, artists find themselves inexperienced and not ready for prime time. The point of the song is that they are not Jesus who can walk on water and they are a lamb for the slaughter. It could have happened to Hunter 'but for the grace of God'. It is a warning not to push the limits too soon. Hunter says this is not a favourite of his. He did have similar thoughts about the New York Dolls, and they could have been bigger if they were allowed to develop and not pushed too soon.

'23A Swan Hill'

Hunter memorialised how he left his family during his teenage years when conflict with his family came to a head. '23A Swan Hill' is the address of his teenage home in Shrewsbury above a police station where his father was the Station Sergeant. Ian left home at sixteen years old and went to Butlins, and the home is behind the Music Hall in Shrewsbury. 23A is still there, including the piano when Hunter visited the current family who lives there, and the Priory School that Ian attended is a ten-minute walk away.

In those days, policemen got free housing, electricity, and coal while Ian notes in concert that 'my Dad was real mean'. The theme was reprised in both 'Ships' and 'No Hard Feelings', and his father did not approve of his son's artistic direction, in contrast to his 'grand-dad', referenced in 'Cleveland Rocks' as 'he was a rocker and I am, too'. The family struggled and Hunter makes an analogy of life as a cop's son to the music business, since the business plan of Motown and MainMan was to provide just enough support to survive. However, the figure in the song who accused Ian of stealing a poem he had written was not his father but an unsympathetic teacher.

'23A Swan Hill' is one of the most biographical songs in Ian Hunter's catalogue. It was the idea of Kjetil Bjerkestrand to interject a sample from Norwegian Romantic composer Edvard Grieg.

'Michael Picasso'

In August 1993, Hunter performed with Ricky Byrd on the Hamn Rock (Harbour Rock) tour while Ian and Byrd appeared as guests of The Mats Ronander Band at Stockholm's Melody Club, where Hunter first played a new song, 'Michael Picasso', a tribute to Ronson. This heartfelt tribute to close mate Ronson is quiet, reflective, and subdued as appropriate to the subject matter. Songs like this are hard to compose since they are personal, emotional, and difficult to say without sounding trite, but Hunter pulls it off with this track. The two mates had a long professional, family, and personal life together and it is quite an accomplishment to say so much in so little time. He sums up Mick in one word and that is 'artistry', so the reference to Picasso is aptly made.

The studio setting, featuring only lead voice, soft guitars and light orchestration, is an authentic, emotional eulogy to a musical mate and cherished friend. In the studio, it took three and a half days to get the ideal take.

'Open My Eyes' (Hunter/Bath)
'Open My Eyes' is a co-written song with Darrell Bath (guitar). Bath found it on a tape of jams from Ian's house and he refined it with his lead part before the final version.

This fine ballad is a NYC reflection as viewed from the Hunters' ninth-floor waterside home on Kips Bay, overlooking the East River. Ian contrasts the panoramic light and sinister dark of the city, punctuated by lyrical insight about the avenue of dead umbrellas and a brolly salesman on 23rd and Second Avenue. This underrated track almost smells of the city amid the gentle musical atmosphere, which is 'funky town', 'Bellevue', which is associated with mentally disturbed people, and 'Imus', which is a reference to DJ Don Imus WFAN radio. Imus was an American radio personality, television show host, recording artist, and author. It contains incredible imagery and wordplay, while Hunter simply relates that it is an observation about Manhattan written from his apartment on 25th Street.

'The Artful Dodger'
The title track of the LP was recorded in 1995, and Ian starts the tune with a spy reference as he used in 'American Spy' but takes it in an entirely different direction. Here, he is a bit of a scamp trying to score with a woman in a bar. The woman is having G 'n Ts, which is a shortening of gin and tonic, a cocktail made out of gin and tonic water. The dysfunctional Artful Dodger, Jack Dawkins, is a rogue character in Charles Dickens's 1838 novel *Oliver Twist*. The Artful Dodger hopes drinking will do the trick since she's drinking heavily. The song is a fun tune and one of few straightforward macho-type tracks that Hunter has written. They go back to a flat for a romp. It's a change of pace and occasionally, Hunter has released simply humorous songs such as 'Skeletons (In Your Closet)', and 'The Artful Dodger' is in that vein and no more serious than picking up a woman in a bar and having sex. Darrell Bath is the Artful Dodger and the track was released as a single and included the non-album track 'F*ck It Up' on the flip side.

'Skeletons (In Your Closet)' (Hunter/Bath/Plain)
The 'Skeletons (In Your Closet)' humorous song would not be out of place on *Ian Hunter's Dirty Laundry*, and not surprisingly, was a leftover from that effort, and co-writers include collaborators Darrel Bath and Honest

John Plain. The song is a bit out of place on the CD, but at the time, Hunter favoured the song's placement. The incessant interest of the paparazzi is the critique here and all the dirt they can gather on the rich and famous. Once the media gets a hold of juicy tidbits, they want to spread the skeletons in your closet to the public. This is the stuff of tabloid journalism, or snarky talk shows both in the States and across the pond. It's a fun song with a serious point. The light-hearted vocals conveyed sexual undertones and scandal, innuendo, lurid tales, and gossip, all pursued by the gutter press.

'Still The Same'

The closing song, 'Still The Same' is one that seems like a lost love and the pain that accompanies that loss. It is the great question of what if? How am I supposed to go on if my love is still the same? If love is right, it's the greatest feeling in the world, but if the lover leaves you in the dust, you are stuck in the same emotional place you have been. People change, and if the lover does not feel the same and responds in kind, you are left in the lurch. The song is a reminder of pain and feeling the same, although the lover has moved on. It's a terrific song about a breakup. Hunter thinks it has good lyrics and it's just a love song.

Related Songs
'F*ck It Up'

The album was released in the UK on 21 April 1997 on the Citadel label (CIT1CD); the title track was released as a single on the same day (CIT101CDS). This single included the non-album track 'F*ck It Up', which was also a bonus track on the reissue.

Hunter was inspired to write the song as he had read a newspaper article about the outrageous Texan P.J. Proby and kept him in mind, i.e. on the *Strings Attached* effort. He thought of Proby as a wonderful scamp and loved the arrogance of his Top Ten hit 'Somewhere'. Ian wore out jukeboxes in pubs in Northampton by playing the song over and over. In fact, he even met Proby once among a large gathering of leather-clad rockers and admired him because he didn't play any games; he was the real deal.

The first verse is to be taken with a grain of salt, stating that 'you had it all'. The woman who messed everything up had a semi-detached house in Finchley, but it is an underhanded compliment; the market had a reputation for squalor and immorality. The high-brow reference to Finchley is William Hogarth's satirical depiction of a fictional mustering of troops from the second Jacobite rebellion of 1745. Finchley also appears as a setting for a character in *The Goon Show*, Monty Python's 'The Funniest Joke In The World', and as the background for Iron Maiden's second album. The 'dwarf on the lawn' is a garden gnome.

The third verse refers to three famous love couples and lastly, Morecambe and Wise, the most famous English comic double act ever. Finally, the singer just goes to drink it off at the pub.

The song fits perfectly as a B-side, almost a throwaway, sung semi-serious and vulgar.

Conclusion

The project was issued in September 1996 by Polydor Records, but only in Norway. Seven months later, Citadel Records released the tracks as a picture disc CD in Britain, followed by a box set containing a gatefold LP and Hunter's *Diary Of A Rock 'N' Roll Star* presented as a cloth-bound 1972 desk diary. 'Michael Picasso' and 'The Artful Dodger' appeared as singles, the latter featuring the non-album 'F*ck it Up'.

Off the radar for some time, the press reviews were few but mostly laudatory.

A thirty-date British tour from April to June 1997 was set to promote the release with drummer Alan Young, keyboardist Ian Gibbons, guitarists Paul Cuddeford, bassist Paul Francis, and the ever-present Darrell Bath. Later appearances came from September to November. Hunter began to perform a new song, 'Salvation' live, but didn't record a studio version as he was saving it as the last track on his last CD, fuelling speculation since then that retirement might be soon.

There were three VH1 television appearances during May, and Hunter did the channel's *My Top Ten,* focusing on his favourite recent releases, and for *Take It To The Bridge* he recorded 'Michael Picasso' and 'Irene Wilde'.

Hunter leads us through a captivating transition from the enchanting world of *The Artful Dodger* to the unapologetic and politically charged British landscape of *Rant*. From the infectious groove of 'Still Love Rock And Roll' to the introspective environment of 'Purgatory', each track becomes a rallying cry for justice and a call to action. Hunter shines a spotlight on the injustices of the world, challenging listeners to question the status quo. From scathing political commentary to personal introspection, Hunter's music becomes a vessel for change, inspiring and provoking thought.

Rant

Personnel:
Ian Hunter: vocals, keyboards, harmonica, acoustic guitar, piano, backing vocals
Andy York: electric guitar, mandoguitar, groove box, autoharp, organ, zither, keyboards, mandolin, bass, backing vocals
Steve Holley: drums, percussion
Robbie Alter: guitars, bass, piano
Tommy Mandel: organ, keyboards, loops
Mickey Curry: drums
John Conte: bass
Rich Pagano: backing vocals, bongos, drums
James Mastro: six-string fuzz bass, mandolin, electric slide, electric 12-string, acoustic 12-string
Dane Clark: drums
Doug Petty: organ, keyboards
Jesse Hunter Patterson: gang vocals
Lisa Ronson: gang vocals
Willie Nile: gang vocals
Rick Tedesco: guitar, gang vocals
Produced at: New Calcutta, New York City, by Andy York and Ian Hunter
Release date: 21 April 2001
Running time: 56:47
Current edition: Papillion (UK), Repertoire (Europe), Fuel2000 (North America)
Highest chart places: Did not chart

The sheer brilliance of tracks like 'Ripoff', 'Morons', and 'Death Of A Nation' left no doubt that Hunter's creativity was nowhere near his swan song, as he described in the lyrics of 'Salvation'. But what truly sets this release apart is the incredible line-up of musicians and a producer who join forces, forming the core of The Rand Band. Drummer extraordinaire Steve Holley, affectionately known as 'Mr. Comfort' or 'Rhino', brings his unparalleled rhythm to the mix, while the dynamic guitar duo of Andy York and the Grecian urn James Mastro electrify every note with their exceptional skills. With the tragic loss of Ronson, Hunter had some big shoes to fill, and fill them he did, as this remarkable trio surpasses even the legendary Hunter Ronson partnership in terms of longevity. The mastermind behind the production was Andy York, whose touch elevated Hunter's music. Ian Hunter unleashed a string of first-rate albums that redefined classic rock. The late 1990s marked a turning point and a new era of post-classic rock, where Hunter reigns supreme.

The songs were all written exclusively by Hunter, and Papillon released the album in May 2001. Fuel 2000 issued the American version in April with an alternate running order. The English release is how the core members conceived the record. The working title of the album was *Worm's Eye View*

81

from a line in 'Honaloochie Boogie' and started in December 2000. Label favourites were 'Death Of A Nation' or 'From The Knees Of My Heart', but one day, Hunter said to York that the album was a rant from one end to the other. York responded that's it, that was the title, and then the band became The Rant Band. The release is both intensely personal and a group musical effort by the entire band.

'Ripoff'
'Ripoff' is a punchy rocker with a powerful riff. The song is about frustration, as Hunter has a perspective from America after having lived in the US for a long time. Ian takes aim at British politics, and although the song may seem critical his lyrics often seem to regret England's failings rather than appearing bitter against his homeland. After living in America for some time, he has a detached yet nostalgic attachment to his native land. Ian has stated that England is about care, vocation, airplay, and tradition. If anything, Ian is angry at the ruling English elite and what they have done, especially Tony Blair. Hunter didn't care for Thatcher or Heath and Wilson was socialism through the roof. In many ways, he is stating the obvious and what others should recognise as well.

The target is obvious in 'Ripoff': 'I really don't know why England's such a ripoff' he relates, 'Someday you might win the lottery/Someday you might win the pools/But that's all you've got to live for', which for an awful lot of people isn't too far from the truth.

Hunter contrasts the glory that was England with its declining state of affairs. The song includes the famous phrase, 'green and pleasant land' from 'Jerusalem', which is England's unofficial national anthem, like 'God Bless America' is in the United States. The song was first performed in 1916, during World War I, as a patriotic fight song by Sir Hubert Parry, a famous composer, lyrically arising from the English poet William Blake in the early 19th Century. Ironically, the Englishman Hunter now describes himself as an 'alien' in contradiction to his stance in *All American Alien Boy*. Ian is explaining how he would love to live in England though he had not for many years since he embraced America years earlier. He asks rhetorically: where are you going to go if the green and pleasant land has degenerated? America is built on making money and opportunity: life, liberty, and the pursuit of happiness.

'Good Samaritan'
'Good Samaritan' is a song with a biblical title and sexual undertones, which appear together. The song is almost haunting, featuring a strong lyric and vocal performance, and now, with a focused band, it rocks. The female character is torn as she is somewhat committed to marrying a rich man but she meets the Good Samaritan who needed more than he could give and not her superficiality. The theme is similar to Ian's sentiment in 'Bastard'. Here, the singer and the woman could not meet again as he asks rhetorically:

82

And I don't know what possessed you, was I just a one-night stand
And not your good Samaritan, good Samaritan, good Samaritan, good Samaritan.

'Death Of A Nation'

With 'Death Of A Nation', Hunter addresses the social decline in the 'cradle of civilisation', and on a political LP, this is certainly one song that qualifies as such, if not one of the most politically astute in the Hunter canon. It is a protest and a love song. The song has almost a folkish tinge as Ian laments the death of England that Winston Churchill grasped; the current crop of second-rate politicians are responsible, but Ian notes they are getting away with it. As Hunter notes, he would love to live in England, but in a related song to 'Ripoff', it gets to him. Ian says that it's about a lack of confidence in the British ruling classes. He confesses that it was a difficult song to write, but from his relative distance living in the United States, he had an opportunity to speak. Like many youths, we believe our land is the best, but once you develop a mature perspective, you realise you are not as free as you thought. Hunter equates Bill Clinton and Tony Blair. It's clear that Hunter believes it is tragic and he still loves his native land and will never say goodbye. Kids in the UK and the USA believe we are free, but as we mature, we find out that we were used, moulded, and not as free as we thought.

'Purgatory'

The syncopated and just a bit funky 'Purgatory' is similar to 'Morons' in that the snobby upper classes are the focus. The focus is targeted against: 'The beautiful people are sent to destroy us'. They have it all, but the narrator is living in purgatory, which is that intermediate state after the physical life awaiting purification. The problem, according to Hunter, is that the beautiful people have arrived in heaven but in this life already. Nonetheless, you have to learn to laugh at this state of affairs.
He concludes:

I'm living in purgatory – I know what purgatory is
This ain't no sanctuary – This ain't no way to live
You gotta have a sense of humour – you gotta know how to laugh at it
I'm living in Purgatory 'n anything's better than this

This was to be the second single from the CD, but the American label nixed that idea. Too bad because this song is consistent with the high bar that Ian hit on this entire release with this song, 'Good Samaritan', 'Morons', and 'Ripoff'.

'American Spy'

On 'American Spy', the rhythm section is really tight here as they were coming together as a band. It is a mid-tempo rocker that never lets up and

83

it has a strong bridge of intermixed lead and rhythm guitar. The harmony vocals are also a standout of the tune, as the voices are in unison behind Ian's lead vocals.

Hunter has reflected on and written about his experiences as both a Brit and an American outsider, and this song uniquely reflects on his Hamilton, Scotland background. As he identifies as an almost-Scot is clearer in his song 'Comfortable (Flyin' Scotsman)' from 'When I'm President'. The song continues his thoughts and contrasts his British-American life.

An American audience would not understand his reference to the 'bovver boys' and that remark would take a bit of explanation. It represents a nonstandard or dialectal (in particular Cockney) pronunciation of bother and is British slang for violence, especially that associated with youth gangs; in particular, in the UK, it is a hooligan who creates bother (trouble), specifically a member of a skinhead gang.

Hunter deliberately contrasts America ('I left home on the 4th of July') and now he is a spy or 'pirate with a patch over one eye'. A good number of Ian's songs are biographical and he refers to his 'fourteen years on the factory floor' as he was an apprentice or worker who kept getting fired or left jobs as he pursued music. He apprenticed on the 'Centre Lathe', which is used to manufacture cylindrical shapes from a range of materials, including steel and plastic. Many of the components that go together to make an engine work have been manufactured using lathes.

Ian has a clever phrase explaining his disenchantment with lathe work but seeking a better life:

Tryin' to get it done quick
I was always in the red – never in the black
You make a little money 'n they take it all back
This ain't the way to spend the rest of my life

Hunter indicates mixed feelings about the USA, remarking that 'Englishmen don't commit suicide – they move to the USA' and they have 'big back yards', 'Platinum cards', and a 'holiday', but he strenuously indicates they are 'Seedy little snobs – I don't wanna know 'em'. Although he went West, moving is just casting your fate to the winds!

The song was inspired by a story from longtime mate Miller Anderson. He knew a spy who joined the Army and went to a bar in Cuba proclaiming: 'Do you wanna' buy a drink for an American spy?' The authorities took him away, never to return.

The line stayed in Hunter's mind for years, thinking it would be a great title for a song. Ian has never been to a Cuban bar, but since he left England in 1975 he wrote the story with a twist and used the same line. Of course, no one wanted to buy a drink, but the idea provided good fun for a song.

'Dead Man Walkin' (Eastenders)'

'Dead Man Walkin' (Eastenders)' is a mostly up-tempo and political LP, but with this song, Ian diverts his attention to a more personal touch. It is one of Hunter's favourites, containing a mesmeric blend of piano, groove box and drums. The figure depicted is in decline and facing mid-life monotony. In fact, it's a sensitive song with hand-holding, trembling, and reminiscing about early days of being together in what is often called the honeymoon phase. Then, the man is now conscious of his mortality and achievements in the past and is now lacking in freshness. The dead man walking is not on stage or on television as the *EastEnders* British drama, which sometimes tackles controversial or taboo topics. Inundated with TV, computers, and video games, nothing is fresh and people are too depressed to think. Oddly, the song arose by hitting on a wrong note and stumbling across a spark of inspiration.

Ian could simply be referring to himself as not being in the limelight and ageing with no one calling. Hunter is saying life is the real thing and he's walking to the end. It's a brutal self-assessment. During mid-life often people are like dead men. Life is boring and often, there is a crisis since we realise that we are past our peak. At the time of writing, Hunter had no label, no musicians, and no access to get his music out. In your forties, nothing is new and life is not as much fun as when you were younger. At fifty, the idea of mortality starts you thinking more about your looming death.

'Wash Us Away'

The framework for 'Wash Us Away' is historical, but Hunter relates it to his generation and makes it more personal by abstractly describing how his youth impacted him. During the transition from blues, rhythm and blues, and early rock 'n' roll the aforementioned reference to the Dead Sea Scrolls were found during this same period from 1946-1956. The wash us away line was used as a vocal tool for melody over the chords as Ian felt the song came looking for him. A succession of liaisons takes place throughout life as we become adults and ultimately pass. Coming two days before the end of the sessions, the clever wordplay 'the heart and the arrow, the rattle and the snake' added to the mostly live recordings. Drummer Mickey Currey suggested a change and it added a great deal to finishing the song well, according to Hunter.

'Morons'

'Morons' is an up-tempo rocker featuring piano reminiscent musically of 'Marionette' and lyrically 'Crash Street Kidds' wherein Ian rants against politicians, the upper crusty educated, and the media for treating ordinary people like morons. It could be a sardonic song that Randy Newman might write. Robbie Alter (guitar, bass, and piano) asked Ian in 1998 to write a song like 'Marionette' and Hunter wrote another similar song just for fun. It was in this quasi-opera style and once completed, the floodgates for the CD began to blossom. 'Morons' is like a Hoople track and covers the same ground on *Rant*.

Eton and Harrow Schools, Oxford, Cambridge and the elites keep the average people in line as morons while taking advantage of them. The last verse is a bit more personal, where the singer will 'abandon hope all who live here' as Dante said in his work *Inferno*.

'Soap 'N' Water'
'Soap 'N' Water' is a personal song that is direct and right on target against Terence Dale 'Buffin' Griffin, drummer for Mott The Hoople, who has a big mouth and spreads innuendo. Just as a mother might wash out a child's mouth with soap and water, that is what needs to be done to this person. After hearing jibes for years from the former drummer and BBC producer, Ian unleashed his thoughts here. The Mott pairing had never been peaceful, but Hunter was perplexed by Griffin's slam against Ronson. Despite the personal animosity, Ian never doubted Buff's dedication to Mott.

'Knees Of My Heart'
As a title, the phrase 'Knees Of My Heart' had been bandied about for some time, but it finally showed up as a title. On a mostly politically tinged release, Ian still is known for his sensitive love ballads as well and this is the focus of this song. This one is emotional and strikes directly at the heart. To wit: 'Slipped the ring on your finger/It's still there to this day' and 'Honest and faithful, loyal and true/Where would I be if it were not for you'.

This tune is another directly written for Trudi, celebrating their early life and marriage together at the Registrar's Office, Wembley, and while upbeat, there is a bit of humour as well. The diminutive Anglia is painted black, but it still looks like a stroller or baby carriage. And Hunter got some flak for the line about a 'house with a burglar alarm system', but he loves it and it works for the setting by the river with hummingbirds, which fits pastorally and peacefully with a home that can be imagined as upstate New York, or Connecticut, USA. The song also came from a wrong note when Hunter was performing 'No One', but it provided the idea for this tune.

'No One'
The closing song (US version), 'No One', about loneliness on this first-rate CD, ends the effort on a strong note. This is one of the most sensitive and heartfelt ballads Ian has ever written. It is an emotional rush to feel as though your life is dedicated to one special love and Hunter pulls that remarkable feat off with this impressive song.

Oddly, the song comes from writing a wrong note because, as Ian was writing this song, he hit a wrong note. He continued to write and 'Dead Man Walkin' came as a result. Thereafter, producer Andy York heard 'No One' on a cassette tape and he suggested recording this tune as well. Thanks, Andy!

'Still Love Rock 'N' Roll'

Depending on which version you have, US or UK, determines the placement of 'Still Love Rock 'N' Roll', which could be last or first on the CD. At first, this was considered as a bonus track. In either the UK or UK release, this song is a nod to early rock 'n' roll and music that inspired Hunter in the first place; it is a mid-tempo rocker wherein Chuck Berry meets Little Richard and could be a great opening for a live set. Hunter tips his hat as a tribute to the early greats of rock 'n' roll when the style was invented. It gave his life meaning and he respects their achievements.

Ian describes the environment of the 1950s, which was comparatively bland, especially in the UK, and then, rock! This is certainly autobiographical ... 'It's the only way – I know how to say what's on my mind'.

Tommy Steele is regarded as Britain's first teen idol and rock 'n' roll star and here he is depicted singing a Guy Mitchell song, who was well-known in the 1950s as an American pop star. Lubbock is mentioned as a reference to Buddy Holly, Memphis as home to the birthplace of rock 'n' roll, and Macon as a note about Little Richard. Rock 'n' roll pioneers Billy Fury, Little Richard, Tommy Steele, and Gene Vincent played the Kettering Granada in England.

You have to love the finishing thought about how the 1950s are better than the contemporary world:

I get up every morning – I put the coffee on the stove
The computer's gone – the turntable's on
I can't believe it's 2001 – God, I must be knockin' on
But I still love rock 'n' roll, I still love rock 'n' roll.

As an opening track, 'Still Love Rock 'N' Roll' is a nod to the music that inspired Ian in the first place. A great mid-tempo rocker, Chuck Berry meets Little Richard, covering all points in between but with a fresh perspective.

Hunter sent off a volley of five songs from the completed sessions, but there was no Papillon single released. However, a four-song EP was issued. Fuel 2000 issued a promo with a caricature of President George W. Bush as Alfred E. Neumann of MAD Comics fame. The promo CD notably included two acoustic recordings from Ian's US TV appearance on The Late Show with Craig Kilborn, accompanied by James Mastro. Although there was relatively little promotion, the CD was largely acclaimed by critics and the press.

Conclusion

During May, Hunter embarked on a promotional campaign, visiting American radio stations playing acoustically with guitarist Mastro. In June, Ian played eleven British gigs. The Rant Band was slowly building an audience for Hunter.

In 2001, Ian was invited by Ringo Starr to tour with Ringo Starr and His All-Starr Band, a live supergroup of revolving musical stars. Hunter played 'All The Young Dudes'; he was going to start with 'Still Love Rock 'N' Roll', but this was changed at Starr's request; although he got the name wrong and asked for that song about being somebody, someday, i.e., 'Irene Wilde'.

Also in 2001, Hunter co-wrote four songs with BDS, a band formed by members of Blue Öyster Cult and Alice Cooper. The songs included 'Having The Time Of My Life', 'Love You Too Much', 'There Was A Girl', and 'The Real Thing'. Once you feel nostalgic for harder rock and rock ballads that would not be out of place on *YUI Orta* you can give these songs a listen.

No one could anticipate the unpredictable journey as Ian Hunter takes us on a transition from the electrifying political realm of *Rant* through the enchanting live detour of *Strings Attached* and into the personal observations of *Shrunken Heads*. From the explosive rockers of 'Roller Ball' to the reflective melodies of 'Your Way', each track collaborates with a cast of classically trained musicians. With his thought-provoking lyrics and unapologetic storytelling, Hunter delves into the depths of human emotion, tackling themes of love, loss, and the complexities of the modern world. Hunter's songs are reimagined with lush orchestral arrangements that add a new dimension of grandeur and majesty.

Strings Attached

Personnel:
Ian Hunter: vocals, guitar
Bjørn Nessjø: keyboards
Kjetil Bjerkestrand: keyboards
Torstein Flakne: guitar
Additional Musicians:
Trondheimsolistene
Recorded: 29 and 30 January 2002, Oslo's Sentry Scene
Release date: December 2003
Running time: 1:36:27
Current edition: Proper
Highest chart places: Did not chart

After an incredible tour with none other than Ringo Starr himself, Universal Records comes knocking on Hunter's door with an audacious proposal. They want him to join forces with the Trondheimsolistene, a chamber ensemble of exceptionally talented string players, to create a live recording that would give his iconic repertoire a jaw-dropping makeover. With the financing in place (and let's just say it involved an alarming amount of money), Hunter's misgivings were quickly put to rest. Enter the maestros, Bjørn Nessjø and Kjetil Bjerkestrand on keyboards, who flew across the pond to capture Hunter's guitar and piano skills on tape. They pulled it off with only four rehearsals! And let's not forget the delightful humour amidst the chaos, as Hunter affectionately named the classical players 'Sigmund' and 'The Little Freuds'. But here's the kicker: while the rest of the musicians could read sheet music, our rock 'n' roll maestro couldn't. So, Andy York, the master translator, stepped in to ensure that Hunter's audio vision was brought to life on that stage.

'Rest In Peace'

'Rest In Peace' had not been performed and recorded live previously in Hunter's solo career. The song was originally released as the B-side to the Mott The Hoople track 'The Golden Age Of Rock 'N' Roll' from *The Hoople* LP. Hunter wrote the song after seeing a Bob Dylan gig at Madison Square Garden in NYC. Generously, Hunter gave the band members in Mott The Hoople writing and publishing credit on B-sides that he wrote which earns the same amount in royalties as the A-sides. It sounds like a summary of a life at a funeral.

'Twisted Steel'

Thank goodness for the *Strings Attached* project since 'Twisted Steel' is unreleased in studio form and it was performed for the first time. The song was also considered for *Shrunken Heads,* but it didn't make the cut, and it was not fully completed.

The song is an incisive observation about the tragic events of 9/11. Hunter said no one should write a song about this tragic incident, so he did just that. It is a simple and honest sentiment written as a letter to a cousin's mom. Trudi's second cousin, Cookie, was on the phone to her mum and killed as the planes hit. Hunter rang somebody a few days later and, by mistake, reached Cookie's mum; she could hardly speak. Trudi awakened Ian to see the second plane hit and son Jesse sat on a roof a quarter of a mile away from his job on 23rd Street.

The song came too late for *Rant*, although it may have fit well on that release and didn't fit *Shrunken Heads*. Hunter states:

And if I cry, it makes no difference
And if I don't, I lose my innocence

These are terrific lines and Ian makes it much more personal and impactful:

I can't imagine how a mother must feel
[With] twisted steel, twisted steel twisted Steel

Boldly, Hunter rejects the religious justification often accepted:

This wasn't sacred, this was profane
You took off and you took aim
I saw you laughin' on the newsreel
Twisted steel, twisted steel

The lyrics are much more personal with the idea of realising the pain of loss for a mother:

Twisted people, twisted minds
Twisted logic, twisted times
I can't imagine how a mother must feel
Twisted steel, twisted steel

Hunter says the song came to him as a simple and honest sentiment. The song is written as a letter to Cookie's mother.

'Waterlow'

'Waterlow' is a simple song; nonetheless, it is poignant, painful, and emotionally heartfelt about Hunter's divorce and loss of his children, son Steven, and daughter Tracie. Originally a Mott The Hoople track on *Wildlife*, it was written in 1970. Waterlow Park is a 26-acre space in the southeast of Highgate Village in north London. It is near Suicide Bridge where the family went and fed the birds. Hunter married young and had two children by the time he joined Mott, which no doubt caused a rift in the family. Ian grew his hair out for the band and his music and domestic life were not in the cards. Hunter's ex-wife was dead set against the change in Ian. However, Hunter feels that this song is the best thing he ever did. Torstein Flakne was exceptional on the *Strings Attached* effort and gave Hunter chills with his contribution on guitar.

'Rollerball'

'Rollerball' is one of the most unusual songs in the Hunter catalogue and it has not been released in a studio version but only recorded live here. It is apocalyptic in tone after the corporate wars, and even a woman with a PhD is not immune since there are too many people who are now victims of progress. Everything of value on the earth is gone. Hunter's target in this song is corporate greed, such as that represented by Margaret Thatcher, though the music business is not immune to greed either and it is a total mess. The song comes from a James Caan line 'before the corporate wars' in the 1975 science fiction sports film of the same name. The song would not be out of place on *Rant*.

'A Nightingale Sang In Berkeley Square' (Eric Maschwitz and Manning Sherwin)

When needing a cover, instead of making an obvious choice of Dylan, Ian recorded 'A Nightingale Sang In Berkeley Square' as a sentimental memory about his mother. Hunter's mum always played the radio and the song was often on during the 1940s and 1950s. It is a British romantic popular song written in 1939 and published in 1940, with lyrics by Eric Maschwitz and music by Manning Sherwin. Ian said:

> It was one of those songs that they played on the radio all the time when I was a kid that I just couldn't get out of my head. This was way before rock 'n' roll arrived and changed everything. 'A Nightingale Sang In Berkeley Square' was just a gorgeous song.

In any case, he thought, hey, if Elvis Costello can do standards, why not do it Hunter style? This is the result.

'Saturday Gigs'

'Saturday Gigs' is a celebration of Mott The Hoople and was originally a 1974 single, which was their swan song, reminiscing about the band chronologically through the years. Ian thought it should be a huge hit, but it stalled at number 41 in the charts and the song broke the camel's back of the band. Mick Ralphs was gone by this point, although had it been a hit, maybe Mott would have continued. It gave Hunter more confidence that he could write hits and his songwriting was strong.

'Roll Away The Stone'
Originally, 'Roll Away The Stone' was released as a single and then on *The Hoople* LP by Mott The Hoople, and the song actually outsold 'All The Young Dudes'. Hunter wrote the song during rehearsals near Kings Road during the *Mott* LP sessions, but thinking it could be a hit, the song was held by CBS for the next record.

To Ian's horror, as a big fan of Leon Russell – he even asked Russell to produce him once that didn't work out since Russell was in litigation with Shelter Records – he released a song with the same title, although they are two completely different tunes.

'Your Way'
Needing a new song to include, 'Your Way' was written specifically for the two Oslo shows in 2002 from *Strings Attached,* but it is a song that really fell through the cracks. It was not included on the album because producer Andy York and Hunter were not keen on the performance. Later, upon reflection, they both wondered why they didn't include it. One reservation was that 'do it your way' could be compared to a song popularised in 1969 by Frank Sinatra and written by Paul Anka: 'My Way'. Nonetheless, they seem unrelated and the song is just about the most positive and upbeat song that Hunter has ever written. It is an affirmation of the uniqueness of people and the gifts we all have; think for yourself and put the past behind you. The song is available only on the box set version of *Strings Attached.*

Conclusion
The critics acclaimed the effort and Hunter considers it one of the highlights of his life. The question would be, could Ian startle fans again with his touring band as he had enchanted us on *Strings Attached?*

Ian Hunter's *Strings Attached* evolved into the raw, unadulterated rock 'n' roll experience of his magnum opus *The Truth, The Whole Truth And Nuthin' But The Truth*. Hunter returned with a thunderous explosion of guitars and drums with his regular touring band. Hunter digs deep into his catalog for 'The Journey', and for the final number, 'All The Way From Memphis', Ian is joined onstage by Joe Elliott (Def Leppard) and Brian May (Queen)!

The Truth, The Whole Truth And Nuthin' But The Truth

Personnel:
Ian Hunter: vocals, guitar
Mick Ralphs: guitar
Andy York: guitar
Joe Elliott: vocals
Brian May: guitar
Ian Gibbons: keyboards
Gus Goad: bass
Steve Holley: drums
Recorded: The Astoria, 28 May 2004
Release date: 26 July 2006
Running time: 01:51:47
Current edition: Secret Films/Secret Records
Highest chart places: Did not chart

After the *Strings Attached* project, the next live effort was released as *The Truth, The Whole Truth And Nuthin' But The Truth,* with virtually the same set list as *Strings Attached*. But now the heyday of Mott The Hoople was recreated with the addition of Mick Ralphs with rockers like 'Rock 'N' Roll Queen' and the Mott chestnut, 'The Journey'. Touring rock musicians also joined, who would form the basis of Hunter's eventual Rant Band. Finally, for a special night, Joe Elliott of Def Leppard fame added a powerful vocal coupled with the legendary Brian May, whose electrifying guitar elevated the last song to a whole new level.

The gig appeared on DVD (*Just Another Night*) and double CD '(*The Truth, The Whole Truth, Nuthin' But The Truth*).

'Rock 'N' Roll Queen' (Mick Ralphs) is a Mick Ralphs song from the first Mott The Hoople LP and found numerous ways into Hunter's solo career. It was included as a coda, coupled with other songs, or performed independently several times.

'The Journey' is an Ian Hunter song from the Mott The Hoople *Brain Capers* LP brought back to life in 2004 and shows how Ian will plumb the depths of his earlier band for gigs from this point on. The epic introspective song about London's Archway known as 'Suicide Bridge' had been a concert favourite for Mott, but due to its length, it was cut from the set – we only have this one solo live cut. The lyrics are unsettling and vague enough to hint at madness and mayhem as the biblical forty days and forty nights unfold while the 'angel screamed in my nightmare ride', concluding that: 'Everybody's got a journey'.

Shrunken Heads

Personnel:

Ian Hunter: lead vocals, acoustic guitar, piano, harmonica, backing vocals
Andy York: acoustic, electric, 12-string guitar, piano, banjo, ukulele, Wurlitzer, backing vocals, gang vocals
Steve Holley: drums, percussion, gang vocals
Graham Maby: bass, gang vocals
James Mastro: slide, electric, solo, Barytone, buzzsaw guitar, e-bow
Andy Burton: keyboards, Wurlitzer, organ, accordion, piano
Jack Petruzzelli: mando, electric, Leslie, Phaser guitar, Omnichord, Wah-Wah
Mark Bosch: solo guitar
Soozie Tyrell: strings
Peter Mushay: keyboards
Rick Tedesco: staccato piano
Tony Shanahan: upright bass
Mary Lee Kortes: vocals, backing vocals
Christine Ohlman: vocals, backing vocals
A. Buryon: gang vocals
Jesse Hunter Patterson: gang vocals
Dennis Dunaway: gang vocals
Jeff Tweedy: backing vocals
Produced at: A-Pawling Studios, Pawling, New York and The Hangar Studio, Brookfield, Connecticut, by Andy York and Ian Hunter
Release date: 15 May 2007
Running time: 50:31
Current edition: Jerkin' Crocus
Highest chart places: Did not chart

Ian Hunter leads us from the rocking realm of *The Truth, The Whole Truth, And Nothing But The Truth* to the more personal *Shrunken Heads*. From the grandeur of 'Soul Of America' to the haunting beauty of 'Guiding Light', each song becomes a journey through a labyrinth of emotions, guided by Hunter's masterful storytelling and poetic lyricism. Hunter's wit and charm shine through as he delves into the shadows of human nature, exposing the peculiarities and quirks of society with a sly grin.

Ian Hunter is about to unleash his unfiltered thoughts on the state of the world with a raw and fiery new album! It's been a long six years since we last heard new studio recordings from Hunter, and boy, has he been percolating in creativity. While *Rant* shook up the political landscape in the UK, this time, he's setting his sights on the good ol' USA. With its short attention spans, endless texting, and painfully stilted conversations, modern life is about to face a reckoning. Prepare yourselves for an electrifying collection of eleven songs that will challenge your perspectives and ignite your inner fire. Hunter fearlessly takes on consumerism, crass dressing, politics, and everything in between, all while keeping a firm grasp on the personal and embracing a healthy dose of self-criticism. And let's not forget the album's title, my friends – it's a direct jab at those who voted for George W. Bush not once but twice. To Hunter, that's like collecting a bunch of shrunken heads as trophies. But he doesn't stop there. He delves into the very heart of the issue: a system where the choice is between two crappy parties. It's as if the country is being run by a handful of giant corporations, and the average American is so caught up in the hustle of work and family that they're blissfully unaware of what's really going on. So get ready to dive headfirst into Hunter's unfiltered truth bombs, where he fearlessly exposes the absurdities of our world and challenges us all to wake up, take a stand, and demand better. It's time to shake off the blinders, my friends, and join Hunter on this electrifying journey of revelation and rebellion.

In 2002, Hunter played British live dates as the 'Takin' The Mick Tour', as Mick Ralphs guested on second guitar, which was the first that the duo had played together in twenty-nine years. Ralphs enjoyed some of Hunter's material, especially the *Rant* songs and the pair let the band play the Mott songs as neither Hunter nor Ralphs were really interested in visiting the past.

Ian moved forward. Hunter contributed a cover version of 'I Wish I Was Your Mother' on the 2003 album *From Hope* by Martin's Folly. Then, he did a brilliant mid-paced rocker, 'One More Time', ending with a repeat 'Austin' refrain, echoing 'Ohio' on 'Cleveland Rocks', for the 2004 *Por Vida: A Tribute To The Songs Of Alejandro Escovedo*. Escovedo is a fine musician himself, but he is also a Hunter fan and covered some of Ian's songs. They met at a benefit in Chicago and got along well. Hunter heard that the Austin songwriter was really ill and a benefit CD project was proposed for Ian. Andy York reviewed numerous songs and this one was selected for Hunter. It was recorded at guitarist and producer Rick Tedesco's Studio with York, Steve Holley, and James Mastro for the *Por Vida* benefit album.

As 2004 ended, Hunter appeared on Jools Holland's New Year's Eve *Hootenanny* BBC TV show. In 2005, Ian played harmonica for Ricky Warwick on The Almighty frontman's *Love Many Trust Few* album and toured for three months.

The Rant Band was filled out with the addition of two musicians. Keyboard player Andy Burton first played for a charity event at the Mercury Lounge in NYC. At the first rehearsal and gig, Burton's case handle broke, but before he could grip it, Ian had already pitched in. Andy had never seen a lead singer or frontman ever help. Mark 'M.C'. Bosch, a mate of James Mastro's, was going to call Mastro after hearing *Rant*, asking if he needed anyone, but ironically the same day, Mastro called him first, asking if he was available for Hunter gigs. His first show was in Santa Ana, CA on 10 March 2005.

Some recognition by peers was forthcoming. On 4 October 2005, Hunter was awarded Classic Rock's inaugural 'Classic Songwriter' award. On 23 June 2006, Ian played NYC's Beacon Theatre with Robert Plant, billed as 'We're

Doing It for Love'; the gig was a benefit for Arthur Lee, the ailing leader of innovator LA band Love. Plant and Ian's duet was the classic Everly Brothers, 'When Will I Be Loved'. The Brothers scored a number 8 hit single with the song in the summer of 1960 and the benefit song was acclaimed as 'heavy-glam Everly Brothers'. Hunter also sings 'There Ain't No Cure' on Christine Ohlman's album, *The Deep End*.

All songs were written by Hunter except the opening track, which Andy York co-wrote.

'Words (Big Mouth)' (Hunter/York)

'Words (Big Mouth)' is an arresting start to the CD. Hunter apologises to Trudi for mouthing off the night before. He has a big one, mouth, that is, and he's sorry. What a combination Winston Churchill's disease of manic-depression, the 'Black Dog' coupled with alcohol and out it comes:

> Black Dog lurking in the alleyway
> Alcohol arriving with the key
> Open up the floodgates and out it comes
> Like a river full of graffiti
>
> They spill out:
> Words... Nasty little lizards...
> Grammatical bacteria

These 'cruel little clusters' are powerful images and a graphic description unleashed by saying the wrong things. The Hunters go to Rick and Steffie Tedesco's house in Connecticut once a week and when inebriated, the mood can get ugly.

'Fuss About Nothin''

'Fuss About Nothin' is about George Bush and his 'five-minute war', the Iraq War. Most of Ian's political songs are less overtly political as they are against the futility of war, such as 'Flowers' and civil strife, although this one is more directly focused because of the timing of when it was written. If you review the lyrics, it takes a cynical view of Bush's justification and explanation of the war. Most wars are anticipated as brief affairs, but as the saying goes, it's much easier to get into a conflict than it is to end wars.

'When The World Was Round'

'When The World Was Round' is a song that is not explicitly political but makes an important social statement yearning for a simpler world and addresses globalisation. The original title was 'When The World Was Young', but in any case, this is about the off-balance world of today in that some people have nothing and others have too much. Today, we are drowning in information, but not enough to go on. It is a pop song that Hunter had not written in years. The lyrics are about two political parties, Republicans and Democrats, but they are both rotten and lies while we are stuck in the middle. It has a tad of innocence before we find out what the world actually consists of. Hunter expresses the desire to make the world better. A strong lyric is 'too much information but not enough to go on'.

'Brainwashed'

The nugget of a rocker 'Brainwashed' emerged on the LP, taking a bulls-eye to branded materialism, herd thinking, and the proletarians watching reality television in a consumer society. In the vein of the previous release, *Rant*, it has an English feel to it and most of the release is in a similar politically-tinged mood. People are brainwashed by consumer interests, fall for repeated government phrases, and ring up their ill-afforded credit cards, overly made up, 'twisting my religion'.

> Speak no evil, hear no evil
> Say you never saw it

In English, this means to ignore bad behaviour by pretending not to see it, and therefore the narrator cannot help the brainwashed. Its original meaning, rooted in Confucianism, is to teach prudence and the importance of avoiding evil, typically depicted by three monkeys – one covering its eyes, the next covering its ears, and the third its mouth because it is a pun on the Japanese word for monkey.

'Shrunken Heads'

We're all at the mercy of 'Shrunken Heads' and in the topsy-turvy world we are in, everything is inverted. When you are born on the wrong side of the tracks, there is not much you can do about it. The song was written about a visit to the beach in Blackpool where nobody smiled. Many British are scruffier than they were formerly and drugs have robbed people of their dignity. With Tony Blair, a good number of people are worse off than they were before. With people self-absorbed, it has taken a toll on British society. In some ways, this is a Springsteen-like observation about the decline of England. The electorate and the elected are not doing their jobs and the Western leaders are just not clever enough. An indicative line is: 'The rich get richer and poor get sorer'.

'Soul Of America'

In 'Soul Of America', classic American personages and images are introduced: Adams, the second president of the US; Thomas Paine, the American Revolutionary theorist; Geronimo, the Apache leader; the Alamo, the pivotal military engagement during the Texas Revolution, Pearl Harbour,

97

the surprise military strike by Japan upon the United States, and American symbols of the Liberty Bell and the Statue of Liberty. Hunter fills the song with historical allusions to put contemporary events in context. It seems like he has 9/11 in mind:

And the Manhattan skyline blew my mind the first time
We went down to the scene of the crime
Lookin' for the soul of America

In any event, this is a rant against current political leaders who cannot compare to the greats of the past. The specific target is George Bush. The US is led by only a few families and they are selfish but consider everyone else a terrorist. Hunter is bewildered by the state of America; Andy York assisted in picking out verses to include on the track.

'How's Your House'

Hunter does release songs with a sense of humour and 'How's Your House' is one that is a fun-filled piano and rollicking lament on behalf of the victims of Hurricane Katrina in 2005. The title came from the flood-resident victims.

'If FEMA won't help me, I know the Good Book will', and an authentic touch is added with the regional phrasing of 'ax' me, instead of the more proper 'ask me', while the house is being washed away. This is social satire and humour used effectively on behalf of the unfortunate people in New Orleans. Another interesting twist with the spoken line ending: 'I don't know, maybe it needs a bridge or something'.

The failures of levees and floodwalls during Katrina are considered by experts to be the worst engineering disaster in the history of the United States. By 31 August 2005, 80% of New Orleans was flooded, with some parts under 15 feet (4.6 m) of water. In short, this is one of Ian's not directly political but socially aware songs done in a humorous and easy-to-digest fashion.

The song came quickly in only ten minutes and Hunter thought the Rant Band might not like it since it was only two chords and really only a poem for fun. The Ranters convinced him to record it.

'Guiding Light'

'Guiding Light' is a slow-paced, melodic love song which was a respite from the more political songs on the release. Ian's two cents on this invented song is that it is nice and could be about Trudi, and probably is. I would hope he should say that because it is a lovely song and filled with heartfelt lyrics about love. It could be biographical about the mistakes he made as a young boy looking for a guiding light and Trudi has certainly provided support and care for Ian. Love must come sincerely from within, so he swears on the cover of a King James Bible that he is in love and they can 'shoot for the moon together, babe'.

'Stretch'

The riff-driven and infectious tribute song 'Stretch' was heralded by a jangling guitar chord that is scruffy, strong, and arresting. There are songs that demonstrate that the Northampton years are still very much a part of his life, and here Hunter describes one such unfortunate friend, Barry Parkes, also referenced in Rain, who Ian lost and how easily it could have been him instead.

The Dr Jekyll and Mr Hyde reference is about the Gothic novella and is used in the vernacular to refer to people with an outwardly good but sometimes shockingly evil nature. Ian tried to intervene, but all to no avail since Stretch went his own way. Hunter's mate had a great brain and a sense of humour but with a dark side, so he hit people. He had a messed up life and when Ian met his mate again around 2000, they enjoyed a couple of good years until his buddy got cancer and died. Missing him, Ian wrote this song for him.

The term stretch does double duty, referring to a long-term prison sentence contrasted to the rock lifestyle in a stretch limousine. Stretch is the 'pirate with the silver tongue' who went to his death. There are powerful images and words in this song about a kid from the wrong side of the tracks who couldn't turn his life around when Hunter escaped a dead-end life.

'I Am What I Hated When I Was Young'

There are those Hunter songs that come along and are tongue in cheek, humorous, or downright fun ('Skeletons (In Your Closet)') and 'I Am What I Hated When I Was Young' is one of the humorous stories about the ageing process. With this playful, fun-filled country romp, Ian nails the younger generation and contrasts his wisdom to the world perspective as he has seasoned. But then the self-mocking banjo-inflected lyrics reverse the direction of the song, with the idea that he has now aged and become what he despised as a youngster. It's a clever turnabout tongue-in-cheek screed. He managed to sneak in 'nincompoop' to an anxiety-ridden lament.

The song started out as a poem as young people think that anyone over 35 is dead and older people think younger people are stupid. It's always been like this and always will be. Similar to 'Words (Big M)', this was written with a sense of humour.

'Read 'Em 'N' Weep'

Often, the last track on a release is deeply moving and 'Read 'Em 'N' Weep' is in the tradition of 'Sea Diver', 'The Outsider' and 'God (Take 1)'. The stylish, heart-breaking regret is a touching reminiscence on lost love. If you have ever been in that situation, you can appreciate the heartbreak. Words are not needed when your love is breaking your heart. There is no reason for the breakup, but the jilted lover who has been left for another has love letters to console him, although they actually lead to tears.

Not surprisingly, Hunter confirmed that this song is based on real events along the lines of Irene Wilde. Since he couldn't afford the bus fare in Shrewsbury, Ian walked to the lady's suburb, Cathy, in Meole Brace, and, it must have seemed like a much longer walk home after a breakup.

Related Songs
'Your Eyes'
'Your Eyes' was included in the bonus EP with initial copies of *Shrunken Heads*. This sounds like a love song but from a much different angle than a usual song, as Hunter wonders if he could see the world through the other's eyes. It would be fantastic to understand what the other sees. It's like saying I could be more positive and optimistic then.

> Wouldn't it be wild?
> Wouldn't it be wonderful?

It will never happen, but it would certainly turn my entire world around, he seems to be saying. Hunter expresses a sentiment that many people share and wish they could see the world differently from the perspective of someone else that they love.

'Wasted'
'Wasted' is a bonus song that is reminiscent of 'God (Take 1)' and could have fit the regular CD release if there had been enough space. Initially, this song was to be included, but Andy York insisted on 'Read 'Em 'N' Weep'. What a song of lament and lost opportunities! This is Hunter in underdog mode, which is a fairly common theme of his. Buff, Mott The Hoople drummer, told Ian he made a career out of being an underdog and Hunter agrees there is something to that notion. Ian's early life was difficult, including a great deal of rejection and he had to overcome those barriers to make it. You have to use your gifts to flourish and Hunter has.

'Real Or Imaginary'
'Real Or Imaginary' didn't quite make the cut but was only released as part of a bonus EP with initial copies of the CD. The singer writes to his mother that he is okay, recognising that everyone has an enemy, real or imaginary. In this case, the fright that the singer expresses is his deployment in warfare. Hunter has written against the stupidity of warfare elsewhere in 'Flowers' and 'Death 'N' Glory Boys'.

Although not part of the official release, Hunter is quite keen on the song. The song was eliminated only because the CD was full and already had the correct balance of slow and heavy songs. The song just didn't fit because it would have overloaded the slow songs on the release. Both 'Wasted' and this track would have slowed down the CD too much. The release included those songs that fit together to form a coherent message and sequencing. The bonus tracks of the EP weren't a marketing ploy; the eleven songs included on the regular release fit together.

Conclusion
The release was issued by Yep Roc Records in America, Mercury in Norway, and Jerkin' Crocus Records in Britain. Early album pressings included a second limited-edition disc featuring bonus tracks: 'Wasted', 'Real Or Imaginary' and 'Your Eyes'.

Promotion by Jerkin' Crocus included 'When The World Was Round' as a single and it reached number 91 on the UK national chart. The CD and vinyl picture discs featured live recordings of 'Twisted Steel', 'Once Bitten Twice Shy' and 'Words (Big Mouth)' as extra tracks and a startling animated promotional video was produced by Andy Doran, identified as 'the testicle with fuzz' video, but in any case, Hunter admired the visual interpretation of his song.

The British press praised the release and American critics reacted the same. It was nominated as a Classic Rock record of the year, and the publication's 'Top Fifty Albums of 2007' would rank it at number five. Three promotional acoustic shows followed in the UK and they also received critical acclaim. Since Hunter had finally achieved critical acclaim, the question might be, is he done and will he hang it up?

Once the personal journey of *Shrunken Heads* was released, Hunter transitioned to the adventurous *Man Overboard*. The record featured Ian's 21st birthday story in 'The Great Escape' coupled with the rollicking energy of 'Win It All' and the introspective beauty of 'Arms And Legs'.

Man Overboard

Personnel:
Ian Hunter: vocals, acoustic guitar, harmonica
Andy York: banjo, baritone guitar, acoustic guitar, backing vocals, electric
guitar, percussion, acoustic guitar, Chamberlin, orchestrated, resonator guitar,
vibraphone, electric guitar [loop], accordion
Steve Holley: drums, percussion
James Mastro: mandolin, electric guitar, baritone guitar, slide guitar, bouzouki
Andy Burton: accordion, marxophone, organ [Hammond], harmonium, organ
[Wurlitzer], grand piano, harpsichord, organ [Vox]
Jack Petruzzelli: electric guitar, slide guitar, piano
Paul Page: bass
Mark Bosch: lead guitar
Dane Clark: tabla
Cat Martino: backing vocals
Rick Tedesco: backing vocals
Produced at: A-Pawling Studios, Pawling, New York, Andy York and Ian Hunter
Release date: July 2009
Running time: 47:22
Current edition: New West Records
Highest chart places: Did not chart

By 2008, Hunter had rocked with The Rant Band, a powerhouse group of
musicians who brought a whole new level of strength and adaptability to
Ian's performances. They're not just playing for him; they're playing with
him, effortlessly switching gears from acoustic to rock and even teaming
up with strings for those extra special live moments. Ian did a series of
ten intimate acoustic concerts across the UK, featuring James Mastro and
Steve Holley – dubbed 'The Rant Band'. He's also been lending his signature
vocals to some talented folks like Amy Speace, gracing her tracks on *The
Killer In Me* and on *Whiskey, Pills, Pornography* for Rick Pagano and the
Sugarcane Cups. For this record, the taping, overdubbing, and mixing flew
by in a mere two weeks – a record-breaking pace for Ian in nearly two
decades! There was a solid addition to the line-up – looking really Brooklyn
– and the inimitable Paul Page on bass, adding that extra groove to the mix.
This album took a more introspective turn, reflecting on the highs and lows
of young romance, the enduring power of love, and even diving into the
depths of mortality and morality.

'The Great Escape' (Hunter, Andy York)
'The Great Escape', the only co-written track since the other songs were
written by Ian, is the lead-off to the CD and is based on a true story.
Biographical songs are a forte of Hunter's and this is one of them, including
a humorous storyline that is engaging and demonstrates a sense of humour.

There is a bit of poetic license, but the occasion was about a bunch of guys who wanted to attack Ian after a gig. These were 'seriously heavy, dangerous people'. Hunter took off with a chef buddy of his in his 'Austin Metropolitan'. Ian and producer Andy York wrote the tune about Ian's 21st birthday. The local thug with the 'best left hook in the business' was after blood once Ian 'sullied' the character's reputation. As our hero is in danger, there is a pop culture reference to his heart pulsing like a funny car, which is a type of drag racing vehicle. Hunter left his belongings behind while he ducked into the loo and instead of returning, Ian flew away, never to be caught. When the other guy is a bigger ruffian, here is guidance about what needs to be done: the great escape. Get out!

After the two preceding more political CDs, this release is more personal and Ian's tales of the rougher life from places such as his youth in Northampton. This opening track harmonises closely with the title track, stating: 'They say crime doesn't pay, well take a walk down my way'.

There is a clever line about discretion being the better part of valour: 'The winners are losers, the losers are covered in blood and they can't get it off'.

It's not a good idea to fight even if you win since you are a loser, and if you fight and lose, then you are covered in blood, never to lose that stain. Hunter is suggesting fleeing is better than fighting, regardless of if you are a winner or a loser. Just to get your proper revenge, Ian cleverly adds: 'I seen his eyes when I gave him the finger'.

This was Hunter's Alamo, the 1836 pivotal military engagement during the Texas Revolution, and the end as the operatic expression 'I heard the fat lady singing' and as dangerous youth fades away, it's a 'stone age daydream'. It's a clever, funny, and entertaining tale.

'Arms And Legs'

'Arms And Legs' is a catchy, heartfelt love song, about which, Ian says is 'A good song!' It is, and he is honest with his work when some songs don't make it, but this one does. It's a song of being all in at 100% and you've given the relationship your all. The deftly structured track possesses a killer chorus describing 'a ghostly shadow of a man', unsteady on his feet, pondering a lost opportunity, performed in a most reflective manner.

This release is one of those that should have been a hit; it is a sensitive love song that Ian excels at. Hunter has enough maturity to be self-reflective, vulnerable, and sensitive all at the same time.

Ian confesses that his poor, unfocused sleep is caused by not taking a chance since he 'walked away from love'. He questions himself: 'I don't know what I was thinking of'.

Yet, he emboldens himself and looks for a second chance, repeating: 'If you want to know what love is', he is saying hey, here I am! The core of the song is exemplified in the lines, 'I wanna be where you are, I wanna do what you do, 'Cause nothing really matters but you'. Hunter convincingly exclaims that the beloved is his 'illness' and 'disease'. He continues: 'You're up there on that pedestal and I'm down here on my knees. You are my obsession every waking hour. All I do is think of you, wondering where you are'. Hunter plumbs the depths of emotion and not only expresses his love but also romantically embraces this love. Talk about a turnaround!

The song still seems to be about unrequited love despite his devotion since he is 'watching from a distance, can't believe you're smiling without me'. The singer asks for that second chance because he repeats the conditional clause, 'If you want to know what love is', I am available.

Hunter hits some high points in his lyrical creativity that reminds me of the classic Temptations hit 'Just My Imagination (Running Away With Me)' written by Norman Whitfield and Barrett Strong from 1971, as in both songs, the singer doesn't even really know the object of his affection. Ian sings:

> I still got your picture hanging in my soul
> Every time I look at it tears start to roll
> I still got your laughter buried in my brain
> Every time I hear it I start tearing up again
> I'm the guy you never seemed to notice
> A passer-by, our eyes never meet.

The song should have been a huge hit. It is a classic in its own right.

'Up And Running'

'Up And Running' expresses the difference between the rich and poor, which is consistently a concern for Hunter. This is a strong guitar track that could be done well live and is reminiscent of 'Arms And Legs'. The song appears to be about someone who is down and out but seeking to get up and running. Yes, the world is off-kilter, but interestingly, Hunter invokes the Mott The Hoople juice as a band that was down and out yet fought back. It's a 'you can do it' type of statement. Ian says of it that it is an underdog song, it certainly is, and life is easier when you have money.

'Man Overboard'

The title track was originally entitled 'Drunk And Disorderly', but it is a powerful treatise on the life of the person left behind and living a miserable existence. The acoustic-based anecdote visualises alcohol rather than seawater, overwhelming this dejected individual. The derelict was not born in booze but sunk in it as he tried to wash away his internalised anger. Poverty and the sense of hopelessness fill this track and emotionally tug at us to hear of a down-and-out life. The picture painted was a downbeat snapshot of repossessed homes and crime. The immediate issue is where you can find him drunk and disorderly despite all the technology available to help. You can display your 'insides on TV', but they have not found a cure for the narrator. Ian references Dante Alighieri's work *Inferno* and echoes its most famous phrase: Abandon hope all who live here.

The 12 steps of Alcoholics Anonymous won't work and the song seems like one of Ian's Northampton mates: overboard, drunk, and unredeemable.

Hunter says this is a working man's blues, but this guy isn't working, thus it is an English blues song. It is based on a person who is no longer with us and his life wound up as a mess.

'Babylon Blues'

'Babylon Blues' arose before connecting with the Rant Band and it could get overlooked; nonetheless, this is a first-rate track. This is Hunter's put-down of a self-destructive figure and an unsympathetic critique of celebrity meltdowns; it is a fine slice of boogie-style pop.

This is a female academic who is pulling the singer down. She is nothing but bad news and there are no identifiable clues to indicate if this is from personal experience or a more general observation of the declining state of higher education. Whatever the situation, it is evil; hence, the reference to Babylon is appropriate and the lyrics raise the possibility of implicit anger. It is a strongly worded and powerful diatribe.

'Girl From The Office'

This early youthful years tale is a story of lust and bravado. The song is delivered with acoustic and bouzouki instrumentation about an actual incident. Ian worked on the factory floor and he relates a working-class roots romance tale with this song. He was a '16-year-old apprentice covered in filth'. It is reminiscent of the Kinks and feels English. The older men wolf-whistle and the boys just drool. The girl worked at Sentinel in Shrewsbury and her name is Margaret Oliver, and you can imagine the scene with these grungy guys and the clean-looking girl. Ian seized this opportunity and learned that she enjoyed dancing. He enrolled in the Sabrina Dancing Academy as his way to be somebody; yes, a juvenile dream. Nonetheless, it has a happy ending (he gets the girl), so clearly, this tale is just the opposite of 'Irene Wilde'. Ian did become a 'happening dude' and it is a true story. For a juvenile story, Ian was quite the gentleman because when he is pressed for information about the particulars, he says: 'I feel bad 'cos she's so sweet and I'm sick of everybody asking me'.

A clever rhyme is really genius, pairing 'office' with 'stand-offish'. The song was Hunter's fun song for this release and is simply sweet.

'Flowers'

Ian says 'Flowers' revolves around the line that came first: 'Sometimes flowers aren't enough'. It hearkens back to the Vietnam era and that war is too stupid for words.

This is one of the most ardent anti-war songs in the Hunter catalogue and it is a heartfelt plea for peace: flowers are not enough. The elites who get us into wars are out of touch and this topic is similar to 'Death 'N' Glory Boys' lamenting the stupidity of the Falklands War. The flowers that people traditionally place at funerals are not enough to make up for the loss of life. He says to give it up and not fall victim to the propaganda that warfare is necessary. In the chorus, he pleads:

> Death, starvation, exploitation, helpless, homeless, furious
> Mass confusion, disillusion,
> Sometimes flowers ain't enough
> I can't see God, the trees are in the way
> I can't see hope, can't find love
> Every man killed is an insult to any faith
> Sometimes flowers ain't enough

It's a powerful statement and well done musically to support the strong lyrics accompanying the song.

'These Feelings'

'These Feelings' is a detailed and reflective autobiographical song that celebrates long-term affection. It is touching with a simplicity and truth that is hard to be denied. For some, this song is one of the weakest on the CD, but although the theme is common, the sensitivity and sentiment are not easy to pull off. It is all about love, and specifically about Hunter's wife, Trudi. It is a piano song and producer Andy York added a mystical sound. Ian favours ambiguity in songs, so we, as the listeners, can draw our own conclusions, but he states there is an element of truth about this song as opposed to manufactured songs such as 'Honaloochie Boogie'.

'Win It All'

The melody is well-done on 'Win It All' and it is a gentle, hymn-like track featuring soft piano and sensitive accordion, punctuated with Hunter's restrained vocal. This is a positive track about never giving up and is something that Ian himself can advise. He didn't give up on himself and kept at it in order to have a successful musical career. The melody came first and later on, the lyrics to this song. Every once in a while, one comes along and Ian will write a lullaby something similar to 'Don't Let Go'. With a song like this, people will relate that it got them through a difficult period. Songs do soothe us and make us feel better, as demonstrated by scientific research.

'Way With Words'

One of the keys to a long and successful relationship is communication and that is the topic of 'Way With Words'. The balance of having the right way to express ideas with words is not easy; the subject here is one that is profound, personal, and extraordinarily difficult to pull off. Hunter does not remember how this song developed, but I know it came after many years of being in a close relationship that lasts and ideally is formed with a person who understands even a slow thinker who, at times, can have a swift tongue.

'River Of Tears'

The last song on the CD, 'River Of Tears' explores one of Hunter's interests, which is Native American lore, and this song is similar to what he expressed on 'Ta Shunka Witco (Crazy Horse)'. The Agouras is a reference to the Chumash who settled in Agoura Hills, California, about 10,000 years ago.

Realistically, Ian points out that Native Americans fought each other, but he points out one tribe that was different: they were artisans. The song tells the story of a lost daughter who hides in a tree, but when the village tears turn into a river: 'the river flowed like an arrow to the foot of a hollow tree'. The legend grew about this startling event of healing. This is quite a unique take on a Native American story.

Ian was at a hotel and when the lift took a long time, he read about the legend and wrote this song about the story.

Conclusion

The press were laudatory, and on 23 July, Hunter launched the release with a performance at New York's City Winery, including seven songs from the new CD. The project was ranked number 20 in Classic Rock's 'Fifty Best Albums of 2009'.

Actually, the only thing that detracted from the release was the long-awaited return of the original Mott The Hoople band, appearances that were marred by the physical limitations of Buff Griffin. Martin Chambers of the Pretenders deputised. To critical and popular acclaim, the 1 October Live at HMV Hammersmith Apollo 2009 performance was issued as a three-CD set by Concert Live.

As the Mott excitement subsided, from April to June 2010, Ian and The Rant Band toured Britain, Europe, and America. Hunter was featured on the UK TV show *Later...With Jools Holland* playing 'Flowers' and 'Once Bitten Twice Shy'. In October, The Rant Band played ten UK gigs, introducing four string players at three of the concerts found on the London tube, Oopsie Mamushka, to provide yet another twist to live performances.

Ian Hunter navigates the exhilarating transition from the adventurous seas of *Man Overboard* to the commanding view up on The Hill of *When I'm President*. From the infectious hooks of 'Black Tears' to the celebratory anthem of 'When I'm President', each track resonates with a sense of purpose and determination.

When I'm President

Personnel:
Ian Hunter: vocals
Andy York: guitar, backing vocals
James Mastro: guitar
Mark Bosch: guitar
Paul Page: bass, gang vocals
Steve Holley: drums, percussion
Andy Burton: organ, piano
Produced at: A-Pawling Studios, Pawling, New York, by Andy York and Ian Hunter
Release date: January 2012
Running time: 40:38
Current edition: Proper Records
Highest chart places: UK: 97, US: 151

When I'm President is a testament to Hunter's timeless songwriting prowess, where he fearlessly tackles social and political issues with a blend of wit, charm, and a generous dose of rock swagger. Get ready to pledge your allegiance to the electrifying soundscape of *When I'm President* and let the revolution begin.

An important note with this release is that this is the first of three studio albums in a row that will make the charts since *YUI Orta* in 1989. Hunter redefined the classic rock formula: have hits, then repeat your hits on stage. Ian is forging new ground beyond classic rock. Write better songs, don't look back, and with each studio and live release, break new ground.

Hunter was on a roll, receiving critical acclaim and regaining fans again, and after successful releases, the next studio would begin. For his live sets in 2011, Ian changed things up again by playing songs from *The Hoople* LP and two standards: Ben E. King's, 'Stand By Me' and 'Isolation'. John Lennon had recorded both songs and when Ian was asked to do Lennon shows for a tribute event that didn't happen, he just incorporated them into his set. Paul Page on bass supplied a fresh interpretation to the standby 'All American Alien Boy'.

In January 2012, work on *When I'm President* began. Two other titles were considered, but then both were rejected: 'Recreational Skull Diving' and 'Ancient Babies'. For the first time, the release would be collective and credited to 'Ian Hunter and The Rant Band'. With Ian's quickened pace, the band recorded in four days and Andy York and Hunter mixed in another nine days, so, all in all, the process of recording only took about twelve days.

Live appearances continued unabated. On 13 March, Ian joined rock notables at New York's Carnegie Hall to perform in 'The Rolling Stones' Hot Rocks Tribute', with Hunter and the Ranters playing '19th Nervous Breakdown'. On 1 July, the Band played at the Hop Farm Festival in Kent,

UK. The Band were fresh and hot. Then, in September, Ian helped launch 'Cleveland Rocks: Past, Present, and Future' to support a venture to promote the Cleveland music scene.

When I'm President was produced by Hunter and Andy York self-titled 'The Prongs', Ian's pseudonym for the pair. The release was not as personally reflective nor as political as his recent efforts, but he expanded his insights into historical vignettes about Native American leader Crazy Horse, the outlaw Jesse James and the Civil War. The release was upbeat, with eleven first-rate tracks.

'Comfortable (Flyin' Scotsman)'
The opening song on this CD gets off to a smoking start with the top-notch 'Comfortable (Flyin' Scotsman)' which is a powerful full-paced rocker with guitars and a subtle use of saxes along the lines of a Hoople-flavoured flashback. The record would not be out of place for Jerry Lee Lewis' piano or Little Richard and the Upsetters' saxophone.

With Ian's Scots background, the song can be seen from a first-person perspective. The song is a tribute to his roots and although he was born in Oswestry, Shropshire, England, like many children in his generation, World War II necessitated a move to safer climes. The family moved to Hamilton, South Lanarkshire, to live with his Aunt Nettie in Peacock Cross with his Scottish father's family. Hunter was brought up there until the age of six and has stated that he considers himself a Scot, but he also identifies as English and British (after years in the US, maybe a bit American as well).

The lyrics are cloying and clever as he imagines time with a lady: 'I bet those twins ain't identical', so once Hunter liked the line and imagined a 'slip into something more comfortable', he had the imagination and the verses came easily. It's a song of seduction with more than just false bravado but with a bit of wit and fun since it is not in strict time. There are some songs of Hunter's that are just fun and not on serious topics, as Ian noted: 'It's just a bluesy fun song'.

'Fatally Flawed'
'Fatally Flawed' was alternately restrained, then explosive, and driven by distorted and soulful guitar, while acidic lyrics assaulted the senses with tales of addictive personalities and departed pop stars such as Whitney Houston and Amy Whitehouse. In fact, Hunter appeared alongside Amy in 2004 on Jools Holland's BBC TV show.

The deeply reflective Ian has said this is about the scales of life, which is an image first depicted in the second-century Christian book *The Testament Of Abraham*. With only two chords the trick is to be profound lyrically about addictive personalities, which Hunter pulls off and is similar to how blues songs are constructed: simple but deep. Ian also noted how well Mark Bosch played on this track which helps contribute to making this lyrically and musically one of Ian's best songs ever.

There are clever insights since the addictive flaws hide in a sacred heart biding its time until emerging. And, these flaws hide anywhere, both in your head or a more physically obvious place such as your 'between your thighs'. These personalities don't know when the flaws will hit them as a twist in their DNA. The flaws can cut you and they never fade away. This is one of the deepest and most profound of Hunter's tracks about the doctrine of humanity, who we are, sin, and the elusiveness of salvation.

'When I'm President'

The title track of the CD is a standout, starting from the underdog opening line 'Stranger' from the title of the famous 1961 science fiction novel by American author Robert Heinlein. Even if Hunter were Aladdin with the magic lamp, he could not change political and economic conditions. Ian's intent if he were president would be to lean on the 1% fat cats, meaning the super-rich. Hunter demonstrates an insider's view of American politics favouring the 28th Amendment. The proposed 28th Amendment means that Congress shall make no law that applies to citizens and does not apply equally to Senators and Representatives. Currently, politicians are pirates and robbers whining that they don't have enough money. His administration would be as significant as the presidents on Mount Rushmore and his 'ugly mug' would be placed there as well. Presidents aspire to be great, but 'something happens to you up on the Hill' (Congress). If you try to buck the system, you will be subject to torture, as in *The Pit And The Pendulum*, depicted in the short story by American writer Edgar Allan Poe. Hunter realises this will never happen, so he ends the song with the phrase 'when pigs fly', a figure of speech so hyperbolic that it describes an impossibility.

The song was first called 'But I Will If I Have To', but Ian had no lyrics for it and he would have lost the melody. He then tried 'When I'm Superman' during an electoral year for Obama in the USA, but Hunter thought this was ostentatious and he settled for president instead. It's tongue in cheek and not much changed anyway. The song is written as if it were a guy in a bar or a pub thinking aloud: if I were president, here are all the things I would do: I would be great. The statement is that both the political right and left continue to fail.

'What For'

'What For' is a fun rocker with strong guitars and piano reminiscent of early Mott The Hoople or The Rolling Stones. It's a critique of society or even certain individuals. There is so much trash television, magazines, bling, and cell phones, but what is needed is to use your own mind. He's urging the listener to know who and what you are, who your friends and enemies are, and grow in the big world we are in.

Hunter has said this song is about entitled youth. They have material things, but they are miserable. 'What for?' is the response the young people say to their parents who try to communicate. Ian specifies that it is not about his children who have accomplished things in life, but it's about communicating with other self-centred kids in the younger generation. Hunter says this is about 'precocious, entitled little twats', and it's about time somebody gets back at them. A clever ending is the Jerry Lee Lewis 'Great Balls Of Fire' refrain.

'Black Tears'

'Black Tears' is bluesy, heavy, melodic, and moody, with a guitar solo that is reminiscent of a beloved Ronson contribution. The track has a stormy piano with interesting chord changes, sparked by Mark Bosch's astounding and emotional solo done in just two takes.

Can the emotions of a lover draw you in since tears are 'Little beads of misery that kill me when you cry'? In this case, the lover says: 'Let me kiss the circles better underneath your eyes'. Those black tears can't be stopped and they return as when the levee breaks. Each of the colours is pointedly crying then as black eyes are: 'Black tears, every drop a kiss/You know how to suck the soul out of every note there is'. What a terrific line, but then the onset of tears could be fake or real, switched on and off, but when the black tears come, the lover can get them out of there. The colour-filled lyrics paint a brilliant picture and then intriguingly end on an unresolved note. Brilliant.

Hunter saw Chrissie Hyde at a gig when invited to attend by Martin Chambers, the drummer who played at the Mott reunions. Hyde's heavy black-eye makeup started streaking under the strong stage lights. Black tears suggested a good phrase for Ian to use in a song.

'Saint' (Hunter/Mastro)

The Civil War and the Wild West were the subjects of three songs on the record. 'Saint', co-written with guitarist James Mastro, explores Hunter's interest in the American Wild Wild West. It is an up-tempo rocker along the lines of 'Twisted Steel'. There were all kinds of malcontents following the American Civil War, and people were not prepared for the brutality of the American fight to end slavery. This song is about a one-legged man who lost a leg in the war and could not join Jesse James and his gang. Indicative of how people were not prepared for the horror of war are the lines about:

Lords 'n' ladies, sittin' by the hillside
Makin' their bets on who is gonna win

This is a reference to the first battle of Bull Run, Virginia, on 21 July 1861, when spectators, thinking the conflict would be short and relatively bloodless, came out to the battlefield as picnickers only to discover that they had to high tail it back to safety when the Union armies faced a rout.

The rebels in the song would have run with Jesse and Frank James, Confederate bushwhackers who, after the war, became outlaws, bank and

111

train robbers, and guerrillas in Missouri. Unfortunately for this rebel, who is not a saint, he couldn't join the Jameses since he had lost a leg and would be no help in a bank robbery. As indicative of the bloodbath that was the Civil War, Ian had a vision of the Battle of Pig Point upon which he based the song. This was an early naval battle also in Virginia in 1861. Hunter identifies the appalling nature of war in general and, in particular, the horrific American Civil War, which is by far the bloodiest and most costly conflict in American history. He writes:

It ain't the same without the music
There's no music on battlefields.

'Just The Way You Look Tonight'
If you are a songwriter, you have to write one for the wife now and again and Ian outdid himself with the 'Just The Way You Look Tonight' love song to Trudi. This song is so down to earth but lovely and it is a tribute to long-lasting domestic harmony about a working girl. The song references films with *West Side Story*, people from differing backgrounds as appropriate for Ian and Trudi, and the Swinging Sixties icon and actress Julie Christie (Hunter likes her classic jawline). It seems to arise from an impressionable moment about a particular night.

'Wild Bunch'
'Wild Bunch' is an unusual rocker of a song sounding something like the Faces might have done. The song is about an actual movie and Hunter ends the tune with maybe someone should make a movie about the Wild Bunch! The song is set in one of the favourite periods of Ian's interest, i.e., American events that transpired between 1840 and 1915. He relates the tale as if he were part of the Wild Bunch:

An' I'm playin' dead underneath a bed, listening to the bullets whine

The 1969 film was controversial because of its graphic violence and its portrayal of crude men attempting to survive by any available means. At the end of his song, Ian samples the traditional Christian hymn 'Shall We Gather At The River?', noting, of course, that the hymn was first employed as an ironic counterpoint during an onscreen massacre in the film. The lyrics note:

We shall gather by the river
And beat up on the wild bunch

In contrast, Hunter reverses the use of the hymn with the motifs of the song found in Revelation 22: 1-2 as the possibility of restoration and reward for the

Wild Bunch. Hunter refers in the body of the song to the film characters of Thornton, Pike, Mapache, Angel, and Tess.

Loosely based on the film, Ian took a long movie and condensed it down to the bare bones to relate the storyline.

'Ta Shunka Witco (Crazy Horse)'

'Ta Shunka Witco (Crazy Horse)' comes complete with tom-toms sounding like heartbeats, guitar attacks and flute; the song is tense and powerful as Hunter digs into history fairly often and Native American themes are a topic of interest, e.g., 'River Of Tears'. The attraction for Ian is the underdog nature of historical characters and Crazy Horse is ideal for that purpose.

Cavalry tactics dictate that on the defence, soldiers dismount, but at the Battle of Little Bighorn, the accounts state that Crazy Horse (ta shunka witco) did the same, as noted in the song:

I never shoot from the saddle
Always shoot from the ground
I walk my horse up 'n' I ride him down

The cavalry retreated as they were surrounded and outnumbered, and there were a series of ground attacks until all of Lieutenant Colonel George A. Custer's men were killed.

'I decoyed Fetterman' refers to the Fetterman Fight on 21 December 1866 when Crazy Horse and nine warriors lured a detachment of 81 troopers to their death who were led by Captain William J. Fetterman. The song relates:

The only good white is a dead white
That's what I was taught

Truthfully, Hunter relates that Crazy Horse, the Lakota war leader of the Oglala band, fought not only troopers but also other Native Americans such as the Shoshone, Arapahoe, Omaha, and Crow. As a young boy, Crazy Horse was known as Curley Hair. Later, he was renamed Horse On Sight. During a battle with the Arapahos, the young Crazy Horse showed bravery. As a result, Crazy Horse, the father, passed on his name to his son in honour of his war deed. The father would be known thereafter as Worm.

'I Don't Know What You Want' (I. Hunter/J. Hunter)

'I Don't Know What You Want' is a song about the generational divide. With two of his three children having musical talent here is one of the few collaborations he has actually had with them in a studio. On this track, his son Jesse gets a co-songwriting credit and a lead vocal, and a lead is unusual for anyone during Hunter's career. The song started out as a jam in his basement, but his son Jesse came in and did the vocal in one take. Ian thinks

113

highly of his son's voice, guitar, and bass talents as a younger version of himself with grit in his voice.

A common issue between generations is not understanding each other and the lyrics nail the difficulties between father and son. In some ways, this is similar to 'Ships' and 'No Hard Feelings', where Ian was addressing his relationship and frustration with his father. On stage during a gig at the Bell House in Brooklyn, Ian noted Jesse came home with a tattoo that he was not thrilled with but reacted with a sentiment along these lines essentially: I don't get it, but what can I say? Both father and son care for each other, but that emotion is difficult to communicate when the generations are so different.

'Life'

The closing song on this excellent release is a philosophical reflection of a wise elder statesman. It's advice about making life easier since fear, stress, age, and holding grudges can kill you, so learn to laugh at life. Regardless of your status in life, we are all just trying to get by. He suggests not to take social media seriously and this seems to be all the stupid stuff. There are serious things in life, but these are not them. The song started out as a strong piano melody, but at first, Ian didn't realise how well it closes out his live shows; this sound advice is related before a segue into a signature rendition of 'All The Young Dudes'.

Less obvious than 'Ships', but Ian is thinking of his father, who died of a stroke and how Hunter tended to take his work home with him. He is describing how doing what you love – music – can also become a job with all the responsibilities. Hunter also writes to his kids to do their work but then come home, relax, and be happy.

Conclusion

The album was also released as a limited vinyl pressing and 'When I'm President' as a single promotion, a Rant production video filmed in the basement of Hunter's home.

The album received critical praise. It showed on charts: *Billboard* (Tastemaker Albums number 4) and number 97 on Britain's Official Album Chart. *Classic Rock* included 'When I'm President' in the 'Top Fifty Songs of the Year'.

The live sets were well received as well. In October, the Band went on the road to Scandinavia and the UK. A new band member to replace Andy Burton, who had another commitment, came through Paul Page, who recommended Dennis DiBrizzi on keyboards. Hunter and the Rant Band live is an ideal balance of songs with one-third Mott, one-third solo Hunter, and the final third new Ian songs. In March 2013, Ian played European and UK live dates as The Ian Hunter Acoustic Trio, with guitarist Andy York and Nashville bassist Dave Roe. A resurrected 'When My Mind's Gone' from Mott days was performed for the first time since *Mad Shadows*. The relaxed show ended with Hunter stating: 'I don't know if this is what you were expecting – but this is what you got'. In June 2013, three sets were played in the UK, including the Isle of Wight, despite Hunter's misgiving about festival gigs. The Rant Band played US gigs in September and October.

On 2 April, Ian recorded with Island Records artists Tribes. They taped 'The Man In Me' by Bob Dylan, plus a slower take than usual for 'Sweet Jane'.

Another Mott reunion was set for November 2013, and while preparing for the gig, Ian wrote a new song 'Ain't That So'. The temporarily reunited Mott received mixed reviews. In March, Concert Live released *Mott The Hoople Live 2013*, a three-disc set of audio and film from the Manchester Academy gig.

Hunter joined Mick Jones on 20 November to record and film for the *Rotten TV* project. The duo played 'Laugh At Me' and 'Keep A-Knockin'.

On 3 June 2014, Ian and The Rant Band played the City Winery in NYC for 'Ian Hunter's Diamond Jubilee Birthday Bash' with a stellar cast of honourees. I agree with Mick Rock, who was also there and who stated: 'He looks much younger'.

In July, *Classic Rock* placed Ian's 'When The World Was Round', from *Shrunken Heads*, at number 60 on 'The Soundtrack of Our Life: The 200 Greatest Songs of Classic Rock's Lifetime' list. During the same month, a reissue of *Strings Attached* elicited overwhelming praise from *Classic Rock,* who astutely observed that very few rock artists improve during the second half of their career and almost no one who gets better in the third: Hunter is one of those few.

In January 2015, Hunter played The Fillmore West in San Francisco, The Roxy in LA, and three first-ever shows in Japan. From June through September, The Band played nine shows supporting The J. Geils Band. Along with a festival for January 2016, an anthology to exceed all compilations was planned.

Next came a journey from the powerful anthems of Hunter's *When I'm President* to the electrifying energy captured in his live album *Ian Hunter And The Rant Band: Live In The UK 2010.*

Ian Hunter And The Rant Band: Live In The UK 2010

Personnel:
Ian Hunter: vocals
James Mastro: guitar
Mark Bosch: guitar
Paul Page: bass, gang vocals
Steve Holley: drums, percussion
Andy Burton: organ, piano
Produced at UK concert venues in October 2010 by Andy York and Ian Hunter
Release date: October 2014
Running time: 75:00
Current edition: Rant Records
Highest chart places: Did not chart

This live recording captures the essence of the live concert experience: the Ranters, coupled with a string quartet, playing an acoustic set, dripping with raw emotion and the unbridled joy of performance.

Thanks to Trudi, we have this release since Ian had no idea the tracks were being recorded at the time. The same month, the band played British, Scandinavian, and American dates. In October 2010, Ian toured the UK with the Ranters as an unplugged release and as such, it stands out from the other available live albums. The tracks are a mix of old and new, with the older tracks benefitting from the acoustic arrangement, and are typical of Ian concerts, some old, some new, and a mix of slow and fast numbers.

'Sea Diver' was on the LP *All The Young Dudes* and a live version exists here. The song is written from the perspective of a songwriter. One verse is about trying to get into the studio and the other verse is about being in the studio. At one point, Ian asked Ronson for a string arrangement and he said twenty quid or a pittance. The orchestra leader understood Ronno's arrangement written on a Players cigarette packet; nonetheless, Hunter does not think Mick was ever paid. Ian says it is an intense song predicting his future as a songwriter decades down the road. He was hoping not to be one of those types falling about on stage; he is not and is doing just fine.

'Sweet Jane' is a Lou Reed song and was originally released on the 1972 *All The Young Dudes* LP by Mott The Hoople; nonetheless, it was a staple of Ian Hunter's solo concerts. David Bowie strummed the classic riff for Mott and the band reacted, wanting to know what it was. Although Ian was puzzled by the New York gay scene, Bowie stood next to Ian and sang the lyrics. Thereafter, Lou Reed came into the studio to do a lead guide vocal and Hunter was even more mystified. Ian told Reed an awful joke and Lou just stared at him and they didn't speak again. It was just one meeting and that's it; they didn't get along at all. Lou reduced his music to its simplest components and Hunter admits that is really difficult to do. How the riff emerged from Reed is just as mysterious. Out of an obligation to Bowie's help, Mott recorded the tune although the song was not really Mott. Nonetheless, Hunter has made the song his own way in a live setting and kudos to James 'Maestro' Mastro for his original arrangement of the song.

Live In The UK 2010 isn't just a nostalgic trip down memory lane; it's a celebration of the enduring power of rock music beyond classic rock.

Fingers Crossed

Personnel:
Ian Hunter: vocals, piano, acoustic guitar
Paul Page: bass
Steve Holley: drums
James Mastro: Leslie guitar, slide guitar, pog guitar, tremolo guitars, soloist, sounds feedback, mandolin, baritone guitar, electric guitar
Mark Bosch: lead guitar, rhythm guitar, soloist
Dennis DiBrizzi: piano, organ, backing vocals
Andy Burton: piano, keyboards, Vox organ, harmonium, Wurly piano, B-3 organ, marxophone
Andy York: acoustic guitar, harmony vocals, backing vocals, baritone guitar, twelve-string electric guitar, maracas
Produced at HOBO Studios in New Jersey, and co-produced by Ian Hunter and Andy York
Release date: 6 August 2016
Running time: 45:32
Current edition: Proper Records
Highest chart places: UK: 38

Hunter transitioned from the realm of *When I'm President* and *Live In The UK* to the captivating tapestry of *Fingers Crossed*. From the infectious energy of 'That's When the Trouble Starts' to the introspective summation of rock star life in 'Dandy', each track reveals a new layer of Hunter's musical evolution. Hunter addressed the themes of love, resilience, and the indomitable spirit of rock.

Hunter seems to be just getting started with possibilities; this is the second studio album in a row that made the charts.

In 2015, plans began for a massive anthology but also for Hunter's next studio release. The working titles included *White House, The Last Bus Home* and *Seein' Red*. Early songs were: 'Everything's A Racket', 'Whatever It Takes', 'Sing For My Supper', 'Yellow Press', 'Room Full Of Ghosts', 'Pain In The Ass' and 'Amen'.

In January 2016, Hunter and The Rant Band played three British gigs, calmly acknowledging the recent passing of both David Bowie and Buff Griffin. Ian played acoustic guitar and sang backing vocals for his daughter Tracie and her group The Rebels on a tribute release of 'All The Young Dudes'.

Once again, in record time in May, the thirteen songs on the release were recorded, overdubbed, mixed, and mastered. The recordings took only four days.

During June, three gigs were played in New York and on 1 July, Hunter performed with Alice Cooper, Johnny Depp and the Hollywood Vampires. Ian appeared on the TV show *Speakeasy,* where he was interviewed by huge fan Joe Elliott from Def Leppard.

118

'That's When The Trouble Starts'

The first song on the CD (all self-penned) begins with a 'Yeah, yeah, yeah, yeah' bang and cracks like The Rolling Stones used to. Pop songs are simple, so anyone can do it, right? It looks easy, just like fast food, since so-called singers try Karaoke and you are cool, like 'fifty shades of stupid'. Fifty shades is a reference to the erotic romance novel wedded to the famous 15 minutes of fame quotation, often misattributed to Andy Warhol. The point of the song is clear: it is not as easy as you think to write a pop hit and stars are not really born on Simon Cowell reality shows. The shows are all flashing lights and artificial music, and you are out in fifteen minutes. It's similar to a dare – go ahead and try – because that's when the trouble starts.

'Dandy'

'Dandy' could easily have been a disaster, writing about a complicated relationship with just about the most famous rock star of the 1970s. Starting out as a song entitled 'Lady' with a different topic, Hunter heard about Bowie's passing. The song became 'Dandy' and it practically leaps out at you as the standout track on the LP. His homage to David Bowie, who passed away back in January 2016, bears comparison to 'Micael Picasso' as a tribute song, which must be extremely difficult to write. The songwriter is trying to say something profound, personal, and memorable about figures whom Ian knows both as a person and a professional. He really is able to pull off both the impact of Bowie, referencing his songs and band while weaving clever lyrics to a catchy melody about a larger-than-life figure in Technicolor.

Ian has said about Bowie that he was the only musical artist who did anything of note during the 1970s. Hunter picks a perfect image by referring to Lord Fauntleroy, who set the fashion of his time just as Bowie did in the 1970s. The 'Cabaret Voltaire' reference is replete with references since it is the name of a 1970s band, one of Scotland's most iconic and historic music venues, and at the same time, the name of an artistic nightclub in Zürich credited as the birthplace of the Dada movement. All of these references seem particularly appropriate considering the cultural impact of Bowie. Piccadilly Circus is associated with people in the UK, but there are Bowie connections as well. His first film was screened there in 1967 and Bowie posed on Heddon Street, close to Piccadilly Circus, for his iconic *Ziggy Stardust* album cover. This is a stellar track and an impressive homage to Bowie.

Along the way, we are treated to nods to Dylan's 'Ballad Of A Thin Man', references to Bowie's 'The Prettiest Star', 'Life On Mars', 'Heroes' and 'The Jean Genie'. The bridge references 'Starman' and Hunter nails the description of a guy who had it all: the swagger, the looks and style, and a way with wordcraft. Bowie was the 'keeper of the flame' for a generation, while Ian namechecks the Spiders from Mars. It is a clever presentation in that, like 'Michael Picasso'

119

he never mentions the name of the artist. Upon first hearing it sounds like an instant classic with a great hook, 'and then we took the last bus home'.

Proper Records released the song as a promo single and *Classic Rock* immediately placed it on the 'Heavy Rotation' chart at number two. Proper also released an exclusive gold vinyl single, limited to 1,000 copies, the hand-numbered disc featuring the non-album track 'Seein' Red' as the B-side and was presented in a red and gold picture sleeve.

'Ghosts'

'Ghosts' is a song about one of the most important American musical cities. Memphis was always important to Ian, from his own tale reported in *Diary Of A Rock 'N' Roll Star* and followed up by Ian's November 2014 visit to Sun Record Studios, and probably the impetus for him to record with the label for *Defiance Part 1*. There is a tasty acoustic guitar, bubbly bass, and an enticing tempo to the song. The song starts as a mythical calling to make music, as the walrus seems to be the muse of music since the word is most closely associated with John Lennon's song of gibberish and wordplay in 'I Am The Walrus'. The pyramids refer to the Memphis Pyramid on the Mississippi which has served as an entertainment and sports centre.

Rick Steph got a private tour of Sun for the band as his father had played for Elvis Presley. The 'crosses on the floor' refers to the small, perfectly circular gouges in the floor from years of upright basses and tape on the floor marks the spots where Elvis, Scotty Moore, and Bill Black recorded at Sun. Instruments abounded and Dennis DiBrizzi played barrelhouse piano, Paul Page took the standup bass, and Steve Holley drummed with his fingers. Mark Bosch and James Mastro joined in with guitars. Hunter quickly wrote down the words of the song back at the hotel right after their experience with the ghosts of early rock 'n' roll.

'The Gang Of Four' is not the Maoist political faction but a reference to the 'lap of the gods', the Million Dollar Quartet of an impromptu jam session involving Elvis Presley, Jerry Lee Lewis, Carl Perkins, and Johnny Cash on 4 December 1956. To put the needle down means how record players were played back in the day, turntables spinning around.

The song is much more personal as Ian has always been a rock 'n' roll fan and he saw some of the earliest rock greats, in particular Sun artist The Killer, Jerry Lee Lewis. The music is so appealing and as he says, 'you told me who I was' and 'you showed me what to do', you can believe him and take that literally. The muse of music captured him early in his youth and inspired his 'haunting'.

The studio is a highlight in Memphis and every rock fan should experience it first-hand. I chatted with Ian about the specifics of gouges on the studio floor after a gig in Phoenixville, PA, where I had stood in the studio during my tour. As a visitor also I can verify that the feeling in that studio is lively.

Proper Records released the song as a digital single.

'Fingers Crossed'

'Fingers Crossed' is one of those songs hailed by the likes of *Classic Rock* when they noted that Hunter has gotten stronger in the latter third of his career. The stranger in a strange land here is the colourful historical tale of being pressed-ganged into naval service as in the 1750s by 'nefarious rogues'. The tear-jerking chorus is balanced by the dramatic 'Hang me high' climatic refrain. The title track was not inspired by a specific book, but he woke up with the opening line, 'I was pressed into service through no fault of my own' and the song emerged. It is historically accurate that sailors could return to England and they would either knight you or hang you as a pirate; for example, consider the life of one of the most remarkable and notable figures of the Elizabethan era, such as Sir Walter Raleigh.

The singer is a pawn in the song, but he is not about to complain and has his fingers crossed for good luck. He is a pirate or privateer from the land of the lost. As a fighter on the South China Seas, he is about to be hung so fire away as he had his fingers crossed. Hunter has so many historical allusions running through his songs, and there is a consistent theme of being an outsider but in this setting as an outlaw pirate about to be hanged.

'White House'

The joyful and fun interlude of 'White House' is that this song balances with the other slower and thoughtful songs. This is Hunter's 'get out of the city' song, which he usually enjoys because of the excitement of the pastoral country air. It is actually a love song and how he has successfully settled down by moving up in the world, along with observations about his neighbours. The play on words is that it is not the President's White House, but it belongs to Ian and Trudi in domestic bliss. Wally, the beaver in the song, is real. When they occupied their house, the beaver moved downstream. The song is based on his actual rural life and would not be out of place with The Traveling Wilburys or The Band.

'Bow Street Runners'

How many rock songs are about the origins of British policing? Ian delves into history and must read a great deal since 'Bow Street Runners' is about the law enforcement officers of the Bow Street Magistrates' Court in the City of Westminster, and he lived in a house owned by an actual Bow Street Runner. The Runners have been called London's first professional police force. The force was founded in 1749 by magistrate Henry Fielding. Ironically, Bow Street Runners was the public's nickname for the officers, although the officers did not use the term themselves and considered it derogatory. The song is about a plea by the victims of the time who needed help against the lawlessness of criminals and needed protection. These are the forerunners of the Bobbies.

'Morpheus'

As a balanced album, 'Morpheus' is on the slower, more thoughtful side of the CD. Far away from the 'fast and the furious' street racing, heists, spies, and family, the lead character falls 'deep in the arms of Morpheus'. Morpheus is a fictional character in the *Matrix* franchise and the god of dreams in Greek mythology, consistent with the character's involvement and dreaming in the Matrix. Mick Ralphs said he was deep in the arms of Morpheus at one of the Mott reunions and the image stuck with Hunter. The mythical Morpheus and his family lived in a dream world protected by the Gates of Morpheus with monsters standing guard. The song is about the nether world of dreams before waking up potentially to, as in *The Matrix*, taking a red pill to enter the painful world of reality. Moreover, the drug morphine derived its name from the god and The Rant Band envelops the listener in a dreamy, spacey sound, in that nether state between sleep and waking. Mark Bosch excels on this track.

'Stranded In Reality'

During his later career, Hunter has come up with startlingly well-written and insightful songs and 'Stranded In Reality' is one of his best in the latter part of his career. The echoey, psychedelic sound collage incorporated one of Ian's unique and offbeat lyrics during the 'age of the deluded', stating that people have brains but no batteries to use.

Here, the narrator is depicted on a second-hand spaceship and looking for a place to land. Now, that is an interesting place to start a song. In the second verse, he lands in this strange land called Earth. Upon landing, he experiences baptism by fire. Here he is: stranded in reality. These earthlings believe in fairy tales and their ammunition. As he grows up, adolescence is no better and the narrator finds himself bat crazy. Maybe the narrator can get out, but it is not likely; stranded in reality, there is a loss of enthusiasm. The song is a fresh approach to the idea of being a stranger in a strange land, but from the perspective of a space visitor since, as in Jim Morrison's 'Riders On The Storm', we are thrown into this world.

'You Can't Live In The Past'

From his song output alone, we can grasp that Hunter does not live in the past and he is always looking forward, which is the subject of 'You Can't Live In The Past' applied to an even more critical situation. This song is replete with references and is a sidelined attack on the futility of war, a theme he has explored more directly elsewhere. 'Sally Army' is British informal, short for the Salvation Army, which is a Christian body founded in 1865 and organised on quasi-military lines for evangelism and social work among poor people. Not surprisingly, there is the singing of 'Hark! The Herald Angels Sing', the English Christmas carol from 1739, near the Hope 'n' Anchor, a pub on Upper Street in the London Borough of Islington which opened in 1880 and, during the mid-1970s, became a home for pub rock and punk rock. 'Vera' is a reference to Dame Vera Lynn, the English singer and entertainer whose musical recordings and performances were very popular during World War II. The scene is arranged for 'that little yellow envelope', or the notice from the front that the soldier was killed. Ian sings:

Kiss the toothbrush, kiss the razor
Light the gas and leave it on
Fall asleep upon the sofa
Quietly die inside his ragged uniform

Hunter is saying you have to move on even when a loved one is dead. This is a painful, powerful, and, nonetheless, true sentiment.

'Long Time'
This is the closing song on this first-rate CD and is a reflective hindsight view of his life and career. The two early verses come close to a description of his early career in semi-pro bands, Lynn's Cafe in 1950s Northampton, hookers, and travelling to Germany to try and make it in the music business, which is the subject of *Bed Of Roses*. To get his genuine start in music, the 'lunatic' is Guy Stevens, who was the first person to encourage Ian and tell him he had a future in music. Hunter was desperate and he would sign any contract just to get into music. The sixth verse sounds like a review of Mott The Hoople that 'tripped the light fandango' and how the dream went astray and 'fell off the edge of a dream'. Then, he ends up in the USA. As Ian has spent so many years in music, the song is a review of his musical career and life. This was another song that started with words one day as Hunter woke up and the song is reminiscent of The Band.

Related Songs
'Seein' Red'
This outstanding, download-only song honoured the memory of American investigative reporter and Pulitzer Prize-winning journalist Gary Webb and his 1990s story chronicling the LA cocaine trade funding the Nicaraguan contras. His meticulous research received little support and following an orchestrated campaign to cancel him, Webb lost his career and family, and then he committed suicide. When his body was found, *Welcome To The Club* was in the CD player.

'Have A Nice Day'
'Have A Nice Day' is a bonus-only track on the Japanese CD. It is one of those jazzy, mellow songs that has a spot in the nice-to-have category, but with limited space on the first-rate CD, it is understood why it was not included as part of the original release.

Conclusion

Press reviews lauded the breadth and excellence of the release. Many critics applauded Hunter for not resting on his laurels as legacy artists had and for writing highly crafted songs to an appreciative and dedicated cadre of fans.

On 23 September 2016, the CD entered The Official UK Top Forty Albums Chart at number 36, Hunter's highest-charting solo record since *All American Alien Boy*. Ian appeared be at a creative high point, unlike most of his peers. 'Dandy' was voted third Coolest Song in the World in 2016 on Little Steven's *Underground Garage* US radio show.

Concerts followed in 2017 in New York, the Sweden Rock festival, and fourteen UK gigs. In September and October, Hunter played gigs in both Europe and America. A further incarnation in 2018 revisiting Mott The Hoople included gigs with Morgan Fisher and Luther Grosvenor. From 31 May to 3 June, Ian Hunter & The Rant Band held sway at City Winery in NYC.

A massive musical odyssey awaited as Hunter released the limited box set *Stranded In Reality*. This musical tapestry blended elements of his entire career: unreleased gems, live tracks, acoustic releases, string arrangements, straightforward rock, and video extravaganzas.

Stranded In Reality Box Set

Release date: 21 October 2016
Current edition: Proper Records
Highest chart places: Did not chart

Stranded In Reality spanned Hunter's illustrious career, and the expansive box set is a veritable time capsule of his iconic contributions as a solo artist, rare and unreleased treasures, and acoustic releases. Therein lay hidden treasures that have been waiting patiently to be rediscovered.

On 23 October 2016, the gargantuan and unprecedented thirty-disc box set offering rare tracks, previously unreleased recordings, and video was released. Assembling the set meant culling the Hunter archives for Fostex and half-inch tapes. Ian listened to music not remembering some of it nor even who was on the tapes. The compilation released a smorgasbord of over 400 tracks on 28 CDs, including the seventeen original albums on nineteen discs, nine CDs of rare recordings, engaging unissued demos and live cuts, plus two DVDs of promotional, live, television, and archival footage.

There were expanded thirtieth-anniversary editions of *Ian Hunter, All American Alien Boy* and *You're Never Alone With A Schizophrenic*, plus special bonus track versions of *Overnight Angels, Welcome To The Club, Short Back 'N' Sides, All Of The Good Ones Are Taken, The Artful Dodger, Shrunken Heads, When I'm President*, and *Strings Attached*, with two unreleased cuts. 'Your Way' is only on the box set of *Stranded In Reality*.

The set was limited to 2,500 copies, including an 88-page book, signed 'Alien Boy' lithograph, and a twenty-page replica 'Shades' music paper of historic 1975-2015 press features, dated 1 April 2016. All of the discs were presented in replica LP card sleeves, many with custom artwork.

Proper Music also prefaced the box set with *Sampling In Reality*, a seven-track CD containing two unique tracks, a demo of 'American Music' and 'Sweet Jane' by Hunter and Tribes. In short, it is a mind-boggling set that took over three years to assemble. Ian deliberately released *Fingers Crossed* at the same time, so it was clear He was not done and not ready to release 'Salvation' as his last effort. 'Salvation' appears on the CD *Experiments*; clearly, Hunter was not done with music!

Hunter's minefield of gold must include the nine discs of rare and previously unreleased material. There is an acoustic gig (*Acoustic Shadows*) from 2008, which is an interesting contrast to the acoustic 'Live in the UK 2010' disc. Two discs of rarities ('Tilting The Mirror') gather together bonus tracks that have appeared on 'bonus CDs' of previous releases. *Bag Of Tricks* collected various live tracks recorded over the years, including the 2002 Manchester gig that was previously thought to be 'lost'. It neatly showcases the last 30 years of live shows, from Toronto in 1987 through to Sheffield in 2013 and Tokyo in 2015.

Then there's *If You Wait Long Enough* which included for the first time the 1979 Hammersmith Odeon gig. An hour of this show was broadcast on

BBC Radio One, but this is the full show at nearly two hours, along with an improvement on the original BBC mix. We also got a 1981 show recorded in San Francisco. This is an interesting twist because it features Robbie Alter on guitar and Ronson on keyboards.

Experiments is the highlight of the release. These are demos and complete unreleased tracks from the past thirty or so years. 'Look Before You Leap' is a great power ballad, but with these songs, the musicians are unknown. Thus, it is possibly Ronson on guitar, while 'Salvation', which was written in 1997 but not recorded until 2008, is a great way to close the audio collection. Ian has said it would be on his last record, and Proper's track listing has *Experiments* as the last disc, but fortunately, Ian is still at it.

Also included are two DVDs. The first is a diverse collection of promo films, TV appearances and concert clips from the past 40 years. Disc 2 includes the 1979 Ryerson Theatre show from Toronto, which was broadcast on TV and previously only available to fans. There's also the *Ian Hunter Rocks* show from 1981, previously only issued on VHS (and Laserdisc). And there is the *Strings Attached* show from Oslo in 2002. This has two tracks not included on the original DVD and is a great way to round off an intriguing collection. The *Strings Attached* show is also in real-time sequence (unlike the original).

Tilting The Mirror – Rarities

'Common Disease' sounds cliched and, as Hunter notes, it was written to a formula and, as a result, was dropped in 1976. There were rockers for the *All American Alien Boy* release, but since they did not fit the mood of the more reflective record, this is an outtake and Ian just went on to other tracks. Not surprisingly, since Hunter rarely looks backwards.

'If The Slipper Don't Fit' is an outtake from the 1976 *All American Alien Boy* record, which Hunter enjoyed hearing again after so many years when the box set was proposed. There was some discussion in 2015 of adding lyrics, similar to what happened with 'One Fine Day' and 'Colwater High' in 2005, but the forward-looking Hunter nixed the idea, so it didn't happen. Ian focused on the next studio album. If he had written lyrics, the original idea was to finish the slipper idea with 'then don't put them on'. Similar to 'Common Disease', it was too fast for the more reflective *Alien Boy* release.

'Bluebirds' is a demo outtake from *All Of The Good Ones Are Taken* and Hunter liked it, but the management of Steve Popovich nixed the tune from inclusion on *All Of The Good Ones Are Taken*.

'All is Forgiven' is a rare demo that was issued on the compilation *Once Bitten Twice Shy* and on *Tilting The Mirror – Rarities* (box set only). As a demo, it was recorded in Ian's home studio and although not a standard release, what it does demonstrate is the diversity of styles Ian can produce. One interesting note is an echo of the first line in the Willard Manus novel that gave Mott The Hoople their name: 'Mott The Hoople was two miles from

heaven'. Some of the most unusual and basic demos provide the rawest songs
that Hunter recorded and this song is no exception.

Who is it about? Hunter's mum! Her name was Freda Patterson and here is
one about family life but not Ian's father as he recorded several songs about
him.

'Sunshine Eyes' is a demo written about Ian's youngest son and Trudi's only
child, Jesse. When Jesse was small in NYC, their home featured an Oberheim
drum machine and keyboard. Oberheim was a limited product, but Hunter had
quite a few. It could have been improved and the mix more professional, but
Ian enjoyed the simplicity of the song as appropriate for a child.

Before *YUI Orta*, Ronson got interested in working with Ian again and 'I'll
Wind' is one of the songs that Hunter was preparing before recording. Hunter,
at times, has written with Robbie Alter and this demo from the *YUI Orta*
sessions was recorded in Ian's bedroom studio in NYC around 1988. In fact,
Alter did this in one take. Despite the similarity, this is not the Mott The Hoople
song 'Ill Wind Blowing' that escaped Hunter's memory, but 'I'll Wind' was
originally issued on *The Journey, Once Bitten Twice Shy,* and *Tilting The Mirror.*

Ian threatened for years to do a gospel blues song and he delivered.
The song is considerably different from Ian's musical work and is about
an average bloke in the 1920s. He works in the morning cotton fields but
he also made a record in the afternoon, while the record continues to sell.
Unfortunately, the singer received nothing and he is understandably angry. It
is one of the more unusual songs in the Hunter catalogue but fairly typical of
how musicians are often taken advantage of and do not always profit from
their creativity.

'Ain't No Way To Treat A Lady' is an *Artful Dodger* outtake. For Hunter's
output, this is more funky than most of his work, but he thinks there is
something wrong with the groove, so it is not among his favourites.

'I'm In Awe' is an early *Rant* demo. As Hunter was accumulating unreleased
songs for a Sony compilation, he found old ADATs. Alesis Digital Audio Tape
(ADAT) is a magnetic tape format used for the recording of eight digital audio
tracks onto the same S-VHS tape used by consumer VCRs. In short, these
are old tapes and Ian took them to a friend's studio, where they found this
song. Hunter didn't know he had written it and the experience was similar to
listening to a new song he hadn't heard before, except it was him! It ended
up as an unused track.

'Avalanche' was recorded with guitarist, recording engineer, and producer
Rick Tedesco in 1999; he is also a good friend to Hunter. Ian met Andy York
in 2000 and the pair tried a different direction with *Rant*. Based on memory
by Ian, both this song and 'I'm In Awe' were shelved when the Hunter-York
collaboration took off. Nonetheless, both of these songs could have been on
a standard release, but they fell between the cracks between releases. The
same thing happened with 'Wings' on *YUI Orta*. Some of these strong songs
just didn't fit the release at the time. As Ian sought something new, he didn't

remember the song and it was as if he was listening to someone else's songs! It ended up as a *Rant* unused track.

The Alejandro Escovedo benefit CD project resulted in a recording of 'One More Time' at guitarist and producer Rick Tedesco's Studio with Andy York, Steve Holley, and James Mastro for the *Por Vida* benefit album.

If You Wait Long Enough For Anything, You Can Get It On Sale

'Violence' is a Mott The Hoople song written by Hunter and Mick Ralphs from the *Mott* LP. The lyrics state, 'violence is the only thing that makes you see sense', which is from the perspective of an eighteen-year-old deprived reject who hated all that he didn't have, i.e., love. The song truly reflected the tension personally and musically between Hunter and Ralphs. Mick left and favoured Paul Rodgers for his songs in forming Bad Company. Still, Hunter was surprised that Ralphs left when the band was close to its peak. It was recorded at The Old Waldorf, San Francisco, CA, 26-28 October 1981.

The Dylan song 'Is Your Love In Vain' is perhaps too polished and overdone, but during 1981 and live, Hunter was all for it. It has the advantage of Mark Clarke on bass, who was first-rate on harmony and talented enough to arrange anything. It was recorded at The Old Waldorf, San Francisco, CA, 26-28 October 1981.

Bag Of Tricks – Live Rarities Vol. 1

'A Sane Revolution' is a spoken-word poem by Hunter, coupled with a radio promo. The actual poem is a reflection on the political revolutions in Europe and beyond and a starting point for the social and sexual revolutions that were to come. The poet is D. H. Lawrence (1885-1930), born in Eastwood, Nottinghamshire, England, the son of a coal miner. Best known for his novels, Lawrence was also a talented poet, although his poetry is often neglected.

Hunter really liked 'While You Were Looking At Me' and he played it live, but the writer, Little Steven (Steven Van Zandt), guitarist and mandolinist for Bruce Springsteen's E Street Band, gave it to Michael Monroe instead for his album *Not Fakin' It*. Ian and Monroe knew each other well because there were three songs that Hunter contributed to Michael's work. Monroe suggested that Ian and Ronson 'Cop this', that is, play this song live, and since they both liked the track a great deal, they did exactly that. Hunter also played keyboards on Monroe's 'She's No Angel' track. It was recorded at Rock and Roll Heaven, Toronto, ON, on 11 November 1987.

Who can deny the importance of the Beatles? No one – yet Hunter is not unduly Beatlesque in his music, and yet 'Day Tripper' by Lennon-McCartney is a great choice for a live performance. Similar to 'FBI', this song was Mick Ronson's idea, but Hunter collaborated and as the duo was working on something else in Ian's flat in NYC, a riff popped up. The groove was right and Ian started singing the song and both musicians kept at it. Ronson got the middle part of the song and it worked. The song was part of the live set in 1988, but it never got a studio treatment. Hunter's version was recorded at Rock and Roll Heaven, Toronto, ON, on 11 June 1988.

Bag Of Tricks – Live Rarities Vol. 2

'Rock And Roll Queen', the Mick Ralphs song from the first Mott The Hoople LP, found numerous ways into Hunter's solo career. It was included as a coda, coupled with other songs or performed independently several times. On *Bag Of Tricks – Live Rarities Vol. 2,* it is married to another MTH song, 'Death May Be Your Santa Claus'. Originally, 'Death May Be Your Santa Claus' was a Mott The Hoople track on *Brain Capers* and it was co-written with Verden Allen. The first title of the song was innocuous as 'How Long', but it was the mind of producer Guy Stevens to go with the more sinister title that emerged. The title came from a 1969 art film of the same name, which presents the nihilistic visions of a young black European militant. Hunter thinks it is just ok but it is one of the most compelling compositions of Ian's work and is performed well live. Verden contributed a great deal to the track. The companion songs on *Vol. 2* were recorded at The Life Cafe, Manchester, UK, on 19 May 2002.

'The Original Mixed Up Kid' is another Hunter track from Mott The Hoople days arising on the *Wildlife* LP. It seems very much an autobiographical song from someone who typically does not feel as though he fits in with society. Hunter maintains that this is one of the best songs he ever wrote. Although the LP received mixed reviews, Ian says that there are truthful songs on the release and personally, Hunter's life was bittersweet. His first wife didn't want anything to do with the rock 'n' roll lifestyle and his marriage ended regrettably with their two children involved. For most people, issues of children during a broken marriage and custody are painful. The song was indicative of Hunter's mess at this time.

Interestingly, the Lord Byron line is from *Don Juan*, 'And Byron said happiness is born a twin', which made Ian seem intellectual, but actually, it was borrowed from his wife Trudi, who was a fan of the writer. Hunter was quoting not Byron but Trudi. The full quote is, 'All who joy would win must share it. Happiness was born a twin'.

The Bob Dylan song 'Knockin' On Heaven's Door' reflects the widely acknowledged influence as Hunter's most inspirational and favourite artist. He used Dylan-like vocals to get his words across to listeners. Ian also thought The Rolling Stones influenced his writing when he was addressing the topic of artists he admired. Dylan got Hunter off the ground and thinks he is absolutely wonderful. The only difference was that Ian was using his own vocals to get his words and messages across to audiences.

Bag Of Tricks – Live Rarities Vol. 3

'Hymn For The Dudes' was originally a Mott The Hoople song on *Mott* and written by Hunter and organist Verden Allen. This is Ian taking on the big subjects of life: God, King, Christians, superstars, and the price of stardom.

Stardom means you are in the goldfish bowl and on stage all the time. The song seems most directed against rock gods who lose their sense of perspective and temporary importance. In this song, Hunter relates that, lyrically, he generally views things as a glass half empty. It was recorded at the Nidaros Blues Festival, Kongressal, Trondheim, on 29 April 2005.

There is a most unusual medley of songs with 'Morons/Marionette/Broadway' together. 'Morons' is an up-tempo rocker featuring piano reminiscent musically of 'Marionette' and lyrically 'Crash Street Kidds' wherein Ian rants against politicians, the upper crusty educated, and the media for treating ordinary people like morons. It was released on the *Rant* CD. Originally a Mott The Hoople track, 'Marionette' was released on *The Hoople* LP and released only once when coupled with these two other songs. 'Broadway' is a fine ballad and a moody reflection on show business traumas from the *Overnight Angels* LP and even more unusual given the fact that almost nothing from the LP has been released live. Together as a medley, these songs were recorded at the Nidaros Blues Festival, Kongressal, Trondheim, Norway, on 29 April 2005.

The John Lennon track 'Isolation' was recorded as Hunter prepared for a Lennon show supposedly to be held in NYC in 2011. Ian learned this song and 'Stand By Me' by Ben E. King since John had recorded both. Andy York suggested 'Isolation' as compatible with Ian's voice, but when the shows were cancelled, Ian still played both songs live just to have a fresh change. Although the lyrics were not written by Ian, there is a similar theme to several Hunter songs about feeling out of place; when I heard it live with Ian on piano it did cross my mind that lyrically it fits easily into an Ian set. Trudi does not seem similar to Yoko Ono, though. It was recorded at John Dee, Oslo, Norway, on 8 October 2012.

The nugget 'Alice' is from the Mott the Hoople *The Hoople* LP, although it was included commonly in 2011 live sets. When performed live, The Rant Band usually segued directly into 'Waterlow'. Ian said he was reluctant to perform it live since it was from some time ago, had many lyrics, and he might not remember them all. It is lyrically full. The context is the mean streets of New York City and Alice is a prostitute. The song was written about someone in particular, but Hunter does not remember who. The time period is when Mott first came over to the States. It was recorded at John Dee, Oslo, Norway, on 8 October 2012.

'The Moon Upstairs' was originally a Mott The Hoople song co-written by Ian and Mick Ralphs from *Brain Capers*. It is a full-tilt rocker that was a profane and defiant song against Island, their label at the time, since things were not going well at all. Mott was loud, aggressive, and desperate, so the writing was similar. For example, they write: 'We ain't bleeding you, we're feeding you, but you're too f*cking slow'.

Ian likens the chaos of the original recording to anticipating the Sex Pistols. The song is built upon the manic energy of Guy Stevens. He would wind the band up so tight it was an elastic band or a dog unleashed and they would just explode. That was the intensity that Stevens was striving for. Hunter imagined the bailiffs at the door, ready to take the band out. It was recorded at John Dee, Oslo, Norway, on 8 October 2012.

Acoustic Shadows – Live

The 'Where Do You All Come From' nugget was only originally released as the non-LP B-side to 'Roll Away The Stone' by Mott The Hoople but then resurrected for a live acoustic version with just Steve Holley on drums and James Mastro on guitar. It had not been played since 1973 and Hunter wrote it as he looked at people and his audience in Mott. The acoustic tour live version came about as a request via Ian's website for a song that didn't often get played. The reference to Ralph J. Gleason is to the pioneering American music critic and columnist for, among others, *Rolling Stone* magazine. It was recorded at The Mick Jagger Theatre, Dartford, Kent, on 2 March 2008.

'Honaloochie Boogie' is a Mott The Hoople hit from the *Mott* LP. It was the band's first single after 'All The Young Dudes' and honaloochie is a meaningless word, but it fits as presented to the band and matched the chord run down. Perhaps it is a minor flaw in songwriting, but Hunter was thinking commercially at the time. It is pop-oriented as Ian stretched his songwriting abilities geared for a larger market. It is a song with no apparent import, but it sounded good. That's true, it does. The verses are about something, but it is still unclear exactly what. It is not something to fret about since it provided Ian with a hit.

The song was not performed in Ian's solo career until the Dr Pepper Music Festival in 1981 and this acoustic live version from 2008 (paired with 'How's Your House') as well as the song is included in a medley on *Rick Derringer & Friends*. It was recorded at The Mick Jagger Theatre, Dartford, Kent, on 2 March 2008.

Experiments – Previously Unreleased Recordings

'You're Messin' With The King Of Rock 'N' Roll' is an attack on Albert Goldman's 1981 gossipy Elvis book, which spoke ill of the dead once The King was dead. It has a line: 'You made your money on a dead man's grave', all done in a rockabilly style like Queen's 'Crazy Little Thing Called Love' but more of a flat-out rocker. The song was to be on *All Of The Good Ones Are Taken,* but the demo wasn't finished, didn't record well enough, and the lyrics needed more work. It's a song that fell through the cracks and was previously unreleased.

Ian doesn't remember much about 'More To Love', but the track seems self-explanatory.

Hunter notes that 'Look Before You Leap' is a cautionary tale. There are no details about the song, but it can be speculated that it is Ronson on guitar as they began to collaborate again in anticipation of recording *YUI Orta* around 1988 when it was proposed but not included on the release.

Although a demo, 'My Love (The Jar)' is a good song. Despite the quality, the timing does not always work out for it to be a part of a regular studio release. It was recorded in Hunter's NYC home studio. Jim Steinman, who was Bonnie Tyler's producer, tried to find other artists to record the song around 1983. In collaboration with John Jansen around 1987, it was considered to be included on *YUI Orta*.

Trudi liked 'Demolition Derby' and it is a strong song that could have been included on a studio release. The demo was recorded in Hunter's home studio on the east side of Manhattan in the late 1980s. Ian read an interview about Phil Collins and discovered that they both had the same studio setup. Unfortunately, it didn't make Hunter sound like Collins (nor have his hits). Collins knew how to extract the sound that he wanted from the studio equipment. Ian dismissed his home recordings as he thought they sounded like rubbish without drums to accompany his ideas. A drum kit simply would not have fit in their apartment. One time, Keith Reid, Procol Harum's lyricist, visited and Hunter tried writing with him. The songs were often good to his musical peers, as we can hear now for ourselves, but unfortunately, they were not released on any studio albums. The song is mechanical but is, nonetheless, an intriguing one.

Ian doesn't remember anything about 'Just Want It Real' but he liked the groove and thought it 'Cute!' It was a *Rant* unused track.

'Coincidence' is one of the humorous songs that Hunter includes on an album that relates an engaging story or with a funny twist. Here, the singer keeps running into a former girlfriend that he would rather not see. A driving character was Kaleel, who was a bus driver from New Orleans during the late 1970s Hunter Ronson tour, but he had one alarming fault. He had no sense of direction whatsoever. He was a great person, as so many from New Orleans are. As they were driving to a venue alarmingly, the band would discover it was not there. Then, Kaleel would protest, 'I swear it was here before'. The band might drive eight hours when the actual distance should have been only two hours: ahh, the days before GPS made driving directions much more difficult.

Hunter played all the instruments on 'Big Black Cadillac' from 1985-1990 in his New York apartment. The early 1980s writing had been eclectic as he was in the country. The Manhattan domicile had its limitations, though, since the neighbours banged on the walls because of the noise after 6 pm.

This simple song 'San Diego Freeway', according to Ian, came and it was just fun. Sick of the cold, he is riding his Harley Davidson down the San Diego Freeway, enjoying the sun and girls who should be back at school. It is something like Hunter's vision of Southern California, maybe similar to the locale of The Beach Boys, and he used the refrain using a name, 'San, San, San, San Diego', while ending the song reciting 'Ohio', or 'Austin' as in 'Cleveland Rocks' or 'One More Time'.

The meaning is obvious and Ian says 'Nobody's Perfect' is the best love song to his wife Trudi that he ever wrote. Hunter is not always demonstrative, but his feelings blossom in his songs. Like several of these songs, the quality is not the issue; even some of his best work just didn't make it on a studio release. 'A Little Rock 'N' Roll' is a pre-*Rant* outtake from the *Artful Dodger* release and it came from a single line, which will often lead to writing an entire song. The rockers are the hardest to write according to Hunter. Although it didn't make the studio release, it actually led to the *Rant* deal as a pre-*Rant* song. Ultimately, though, it too was dropped from release and the record label Papillon was disappointed.

Hunter and Bjørn Nessjø, Norwegian record producer, engineer and musician, rocked 'Testosterone' out. Ian liked this track also; I think it's one of the best tracks he's ever done, but it couldn't fit on the *Artful Dodger* record. Certainly, it ranks up there with the harder rock songs Ian has recorded and it has a killer bass run. First, Ian did a demo and then Bjørn improved it as he made his contribution.

'The Man In Me' is a song from 2014 with Ian and a young British band called Tribes on Island Records. Hunter feels that it is too Dylanish, but there is no other way to do a Dylan song but Bob's style. On the other hand, the Jimi Hendrix version of 'All Along The Watchtower' impressed Dylan so much he performed the song live more like Jimi. Ian and Tribes also recorded Lou Reed's 'Sweet Jane' in a London studio, but that version is only on *Sampling In Reality*.

'Salvation' was written just before *Rant,* but Hunter thinks he actually wrote this song in the late 1990s. He first played the song live in 1997 but did not record it until 2008, and at the time said it would be on his last record. There are two versions: an early take and a second version with harmonica, although he doesn't recall who's playing on either version.

Fortunately, it was not his last release, but it is an intriguing spiritual track. Some tracks don't make it to record, but Ian feels strongly enough about it; he says 'Salvation' is important to him, and he hopes he has not been too naughty since this song clearly is all about the wind-up. He is working out his salvation, stating a sentiment that parallels Philippians 2:12, i.e., cultivate salvation, bring it to full effect, and actively pursue spiritual maturity.

Hunter thinks the song was one of the best things he's ever done. Hunter wanted it on his last record, and, in fact, it's the last track for the last audio disc in the box set. Since it was first performed live, the song fuelled speculation that Ian was finished recording, but with *Defiance Part 1,* retiring has not happened yet, and when he's done, Hunter will notify us.

It Never Happened – DVD

Video versions of Hunter songs otherwise noted in this volume are on the DVD The press acclaimed the box set as the most painstaking career retrospective of any rock-oriented artist.

From September to November, Ian played almost thirty gigs in America, Britain, and Scandinavia and then promoted the box set for several London-based rock shows.

The box set was placed at number nine in *Rolling Stone*'s 2016 Reissue of the Year chart.

Defiance, Part 1

Personnel:
Ian Hunter: vocals, rhythm guitar
Ringo Starr (Beatles, Ringo Starr and the All-Starr Band): drums
Jeff Beck (Yardbirds, Jeff Beck Group, and Beck, Bogert & Appice): guitar
Joe Elliott (Def Leppard, Down & Outz): vocals
Johnny Depp (Hollywood Vampires): guitar
Billy F Gibbons (ZZ Top): guitar
Duff McKagan (Guns 'N' Roses): bass
Todd Rundgren (Todd Rundgren, Utopia): guitar
Slash (Guns N' Roses): guitar
Taylor Hawkins (Foo Fighters): drums
Andy York (John Mellencamp): guitar
Mike Campbell (John Mellencamp): guitar
Jeff Tweedy (Wilco): guitar
Robert Trujillo (Metallica): bass
Waddy Wachtel (Stevie Nicks, Keith Richards): guitar
Brad Whitford (Aerosmith): rhythm guitar
Dane Clark (John Mellencamp): drums
Billy Bob Thornton (The Boxmasters): drums
J.D. Andrew (The Boxmasters): guitar
Dean DeLeo (Stone Temple Pilots): guitar
Robert De Leo (Stone Temple Pilots): bass
Eric Kretz (Stone Temple Pilots): drums
Dennis DiBrizzi (The Rant Band): keyboards
Produced: Andy York
Release date: 20 January 2023
Running time: 38:42
Current edition: Sun Records
Highest chart places: UK: 88

It is high time to transition from the expansive tapestry of Hunter's *Stranded In Reality* to the defiant and unapologetic soundscape of *Defiance Part 1*. We are thrust into a world where Hunter fearlessly treads past classic rock, challenging studio conventional technique and embracing the brave new world of recording.

From the blistering rocking of 'Defiance' to the painful emotions of 'No Hard Feelings', each track is a testament to Hunter's unwavering spirit and his refusal to conform. Collaborating with a dynamic, star-studded collection of famous rock musicians, he crafts a sound that is both timeless and contemporary, blending infectious hooks, searing guitar solos, and unmistakable vocals.

'Defiance'

The self-penned album opens in glorious style with the title track 'Defiance' (featuring Slash and Robert Trujillo), as hard-rocking as anything Ian has recorded for many years. The song is about Hunter doing things his way and not giving in to current trends, noting 'Got an 'F' for squanderin' those golden years'. Now that's defiance! The picture is of an ordinary kid who is defiant and has lived a long life doing the same. The song features Slash from Guns 'N' Roses, who had played with Hunter Ronson at the Hollywood Palace on 13 November 1989. They played 'White Light/White Heat' and proved to be an awakening for Hunter. He and Ronson wanted to rock as hard as newer players such as Slash.

'Bed Of Roses'

In 'Bed Of Roses' (featuring Ringo Starr, Mike Campbell, and Joe Elliott), Hunter states 'what went on behind the scenes was beyond your wildest dreams' while the band 'played all night long'. 'People rave about 54' contrasting the groundbreaking rock 'n' roll created at Sun Studios in Memphis and discovering Elvis Presley in 1954'. With Studio 54, that 'was just a disco store' as Ian sang in 'We Gotta Get Outta Here'. Ian says: 'I can still feel it like yesterday'. 'The Silver Bugs (get it, The Beatles, who were called the Silver Beatles at one time) and Sheridan' (Tony Sheridan) were there while Roy stayed 'forever young' (Roy Young) and in the video for the single, The Beatles and The Star Club are featured.

Ian experienced a similar apprenticeship to the Beatles in Germany. Comparable to the Beatles, Ian gigged in Germany to practice his craft, although not as successful as the Fab Four when they finally hit it big in England. Ian didn't get a chance until 1969, close to when the Beatles were at their nadir when Mott The Hoople released their first LP.

Ian establishes his credentials as that one early rocker who has aged well with the ability to mix the everyday with literary references, and 'Bed' is no exception. He refers to what 'we used to call it Camelot with all them ladies of Shalott the people like to Lancelot'. The phrase 'dance a lot' puns Lancelot. 'The Lady of Shalott' is a lyrical ballad by the 19th-century English poet Alfred Tennyson and one of his best-known works. He references Lancelot as the couple are bemused with each other.

For the pop references, The Silver Beatles were a short-lived cover band featuring three future members of The Beatles. John Lennon initially wanted to be called The Crickets, but Paul McCartney said, 'I think that's already taken'. It was Stuart Sutcliffe who suggested they call themselves The Beatles. The group often performed short 20-minute sets composed entirely of top 40 hit covers. Anthony Esmond Sheridan McGinnity, known professionally as Tony Sheridan, was an English rock and roll guitarist who spent much of his adult life in Germany. He was best known as an early collaborator of the Beatles (though the record was labelled as being with 'The Beat Brothers'), one of two non-Beatles (the other being Billy Preston) to receive label performance credit on a record with the group, and the only non-Beatle to appear as lead singer on a Beatles recording which charted as a single. Roy Frederick Young was a British rock and roll singer, pianist and keyboard player. He first recorded in the late 1950s before performing in Hamburg with the Beatles. After a stint with Cliff Bennett and the Rabble Rousers, he released several albums with his own band, as well as recording with Chuck Berry and David Bowie, among others. Most importantly, Young toured the US in the 1980s with Hunter Ronson.

Hunter has kept alive the groundbreaking music associated with Sun Records as the longest contributor, first to rock 'n' roll, then classic rock, as well as his more innovative recent works.

'No Hard Feelings'

With 'No Hard Feelings' (featuring Johnny Depp and Jeff Beck), Hunter contextualised himself historically, first the World Wars, then Elvis, then Ian! He says: 'A pre-war gift, a post-war pest' since he was born in June 1939 before the invasion of Poland on 1 September. Most importantly, if ever there was a song that could be filled with rant and rage, this is it. However, Hunter brilliantly dissects his relationship with his father, Walter, along the lines of 'Ships', 'Following In Your Footsteps', and as extended in '23A Swan Hill'. Ian has come full circle; first, he left home at a young age and detailed the distance he felt, but now had no hard feelings after his parents passing. Hunter is at peace, but the song is not simply introspective; Ian expresses a life lesson similar to a song by Ronson, 'Hard Life'. Here is the key line which reminds me of the humorous song by Johnny Cash, 'A Boy Named Sue':

When I was down, out on the skids
You were there with your obnoxious kid
I will always remember what you did
Trying to make a man out of me

Belatedly, his father's harshness led to Ian's survival instinct, and rejection prompted his ability to be someone someday; now, at a mature age, it is clear to his musical peers that he attained legendary status, in particular with the release of *Defiance Part 1*.

'Pavlov's Dog'

Who writes a dog about a security dog at JFK Airport? Well, Ian Hunter, of course. Hunter writes 'Pavlov's Dog' (featuring Dennis DiBrizzi, Dean Deleo, and Robert Deleo) from the perspective of a dog sniffing canine just doing its job.

The title comes from Pavlovian conditioning (aka classical conditioning), which was discovered accidentally. Ivan Petrovich Pavlov (1849–1936) found the conditioning during the 1890s. Pavlov researched salivation in dogs in response to being fed. He inserted a small test tube into the cheek of each dog to measure saliva when the dogs were fed (with a powder made from meat).

Pavlov predicted the dogs would salivate in response to the food placed in front of them, but he noticed that his dogs would begin to salivate whenever they heard the footsteps of his assistant, who was bringing them the food, i.e., Pavlov's dog!

At the airport, the dogs are trained to respond to stimuli and if a person is suspicious, they sense it and alert their handlers for a dog day afternoon. The lyrics reference the 1975 film *Dog Day Afternoon,* which is about three amateur bank robbers who plan to hold up a bank. A nice simple robbery: walk in, take the money, and run. Unfortunately, the supposedly uncomplicated heist suddenly becomes a bizarre nightmare as everything that could go wrong does. The song then is about a dog just doing its job, but if you try to sneak something in, he will make your day miserable!

'Don't Tread On Me'

'Don't Tread On Me' (featuring Todd Rundgren) examines the issue of ageism. It reminds me of 'Hello In There' by lyricist John Prine. Respect is the key, Hunter says, and the same phrase was used by Metallica in a song with the same title. The phrase originated with the motto on the Gadsden flag, which is a historic expression of American patriotism. Ian appropriates the motto in the song as a more general expression of personal freedom and individualism which remains an American cultural trait.

'Guernica'

'Guernica' (featuring Mike Campbell and Joe Elliott) has an important artistic history and Hunter sings of the analogous manner in which his songwriting works, which is similar to painters. Ian maintains that the words write themselves as paintbrushes and colours inform the artist. It's as if creative people have their antennae out and they receive messages. The actual painting by Pablo Picasso, as in the song 'Michael Picasso', is a large 1937 oil painting. It is one of his best-known works and is regarded by many art critics as the most moving and powerful anti-war painting in history. Picasso's motivation for painting the scene in this great work was the news of the German aerial bombing of the Basque town whose name the piece bears, which the artist had seen in the dramatic photographs published in various periodicals. The work constitutes a generic plea against the barbarity and terror of war.

'I Hate Hate'

'I Hate Hate' (featuring a pounding piano) is a rocker about 'man's inhumanity to man'. Hate is out of date. It's a great message for troubled times, and Ian's line is 'Wouldn't it be great if we ran out of hate'. And he adds you can wear the slogan on a T-shirt and wear it at a job or church. The tune is a diatribe against social institutions that encourage, enhance, or allow hate to flourish. There are two versions: the main version is piano-led, while the bonus track is guitar-led.

'Angel'

In 'Angel' (featuring Taylor Hawkins and Duff McKagan), the main lyrics are not related, but the chorus is reminiscent of Hunter's song 'Overnight Angels'; the song loudly and abruptly begins, and the repeated 'Angels, angels, angels, angels' near the end reprises the original 'Overnight Angels'. 'Red Letter Day' from *Ian Hunter's Dirty Laundry* in 1995 also comes to mind. Brilliant lyrics abound throughout this heartfelt, appreciative tribute to Trudi. The melody fits the sentiment like a glove, and the song is a true highlight of the couple's almost fifty-year marriage. Ian notes, 'It's hard to kiss an angel. The harps are always getting in the way'. The lyrics come from the heart, but the song features signature piano and amazing anthemic guitar chords. It features not one but three guitar solos and the line-up of musicians is just awesome. The late great Taylor Hawkins is on drums in a restrained yet beautifully laid down style, along with Duff McKagan, Waddy Wachtel, and Brad Whitford.

'Kiss 'N' Make Up'

'Kiss 'N' Make Up' (featuring Taylor Hawkins, Billy F. Gibbons, and Billy Bob Thornton) is a fine examination of the 'get over yourself' state of our world of selfishness, self-absorption, and self-centeredness. We are only entitled to what we earn, and not just financially. Leaders are literally destroying everything the Founding Fathers fought to protect, as they will never seemingly agree to compromise, and in the UK, the politicians are not working for the people who elected them either. It's a song against stupidity that Hunter has taken aim against consistently; he is not political but lashes out against the denseness of elites.

'This Is What I'm Here For'

'This Is What I'm Here For' (featuring Taylor Hawkins and Joe Elliott) is a terrific summation of the career of Mr. 'Unter and is the earthy counterpoint to 'Salvation'. It is Hunter's declaration of how he is ordinary, but he is here on earth to create music. And we know *Defiance Part 2* is on the way. Ian is still doing exactly what he has enjoyed doing for decades and although he got into the game later than he would like, he is in his element making music. Early on, he struggled to make it in music from his youth, as chronicled in *Have Guitars Will Travel: A Journey Through The Beat Music Scene In Northampton 1957-1966* and this song is the companion to the theme of 'Defiance'. He was over the hill at 30 but now, 50 years later, he is killing it, still here, and when he's through, he will let us know. Hunter has a cheeky line about 'frolicking with all the young dudes', which is a response to Dylan's lyrics in his 'I Contain Multitudes', in which Dylan 'frolic[s] with all the young dudes'. Might as well enjoy it: here he is!

Bibliography

Adrian Perkins, *www.hunter-mott.com* Copyright © 1998-2022.

All the Young Dudes: Mott the Hoople and Ian Hunter: The Official Biography by Campbell Devine, Cherry Red (2003).

Diary of a Rock 'n' Roll Star (Lead Singer for Mott the Hoople) by Ian Hunter, Panther (1972).

Diary of a Rock 'n' Roll Star by Ian Hunter, Omnibus Press (2018).

From the Knees of My Heart The Chrysalis Years 1979-1981 Track by Track by Ian Hunter, Chrysalis, (2012).

Fun and Dangerous: Untold Tales, Unseen Photos, Unearthed Music from My Father's Place 1975-1980 by Steve Rosenfield & Michael Eppy Epstein, MRG Ventures, Inc. (2010).

Have Guitars ... Will Travel: A Journey Through the Beat Music Scene in Northampton 1957-1966 by Derrick A. Thompson & William Martin, Whyte Tyger Publications (2009).

www.hunter-mott.com by Adrian Perkins, Copyright © 1998-2022.

ianhunter.com 2023 All Rights Reserved.

Ian Hunter: Complete Recordings Illustrated (Essential Discographies) by AP Sparke, APS Publications (2019).

Ian Hunter Once Bitten Twice Shy booklet by Campbell Devine (Editor), Columbia Records (2000).

Ian Hunter Stranded In Reality by Campbell Devine (Editor), Proper Records, (2016).

Justin Purington, Just A Buzz (1995-2001).

Mott The Hoople and Ian Hunter in the 1970s: Decades by John Van Der Kiste, Sonicbond Publishing (2022).

Mott the Hoople fanzine (October 1990).

Rock 'n' Roll Sweepstakes: The Authorised Biography of Ian Hunter (Volume 1): Mott's the Story by Campbell Devine, Omnibus Press (2019).

Rock 'n' Roll Sweepstakes: The Official Biography of Ian Hunter (Volume 2) Hunter by Proxy by Campbell Devine. Omnibus Press (2021).

*Sven Gusevik, The Outsider Vols. 1-8, (1992-1999).

We've Got A Great Future Behind Us by Tom Price (Editor), CL Publishing, (2013).

On Track Series

Allman Brothers Band – Andrew Wild 978-1-78952-252-5
Tori Amos – Lisa Torem 978-1-78952-142-9
Aphex Twin – Beau Waddell 978-1-78952-267-9
Asia – Peter Braidis 978-1-78952-099-6
Badfinger – Robert Day-Webb 978-1-878952-176-4
Barclay James Harvest – Keith And Monica Domone 978-1-78952-067-5
Beck – Arthur Lizie 978-1-78952-258-7
The Beatles – Andrew Wild 978-1-78952-009-5
The Beatles Solo 1969-1980 – Andrew Wild 978-1-78952-030-9
Blue Oyster Cult – Jacob Holm-Lupo 978-1-78952-007-1
Blur – Matt Bishop 978-178952-164-1
Marc Bolan And T.rex – Peter Gallagher 978-1-78952-124-5
Kate Bush – Bill Thomas 978-1-78952-097-2
Camel – Hamish Kuzminski 978-1-78952-040-8
Captain Beefheart – Opher Goodwin 978-1-78952-235-8
Caravan – Andy Boot 978-1-78952-127-6
Cardiacs – Eric Benac 978-1-78952-131-3
Nick Cave And The Bad Seeds – Dominic Sanderson 978-1-78952-240-2
Eric Clapton Solo – Andrew Wild 978-1-78952-141-2
The Clash – Nick Assirati 978-1-78952-077-4
Elvis Costello And The Attractions – Georg Purvis 978-1-78952-129-0
Crosby, Stills & Nash – Andrew Wild 978-1-78952-039-2
Creedence Clearwater Revival – Tony Thompson 978-178952-237-2
The Damned – Morgan Brown 978-1-78952-136-8
Deep Purple And Rainbow 1968-79 – Steve Pilkington 978-1-78952-002-6
Dire Straits – Andrew Wild 978-1-78952-044-6
The Doors – Tony Thompson 978-1-78952-137-5
Dream Theater – Jordan Blum 978-1-78952-050-7
Eagles – John Van Der Kiste 978-1-78952-260-0
Earth, Wind And Fire – Bud Wilkins 978-1-78952-272-3
Electric Light Orchestra – Barry Delve 978 1 78952 152 8
Emerson Lake And Palmer – Mike Goode 978-1-78952-000-2
Fairport Convention – Kevan Furbank 978-1-78952-051-4
Peter Gabriel – Graeme Scarfe 978-1-78952-138-2
Genesis – Stuart Macfarlane 978-1-78952-005-7
Gentle Giant – Gary Steel 978-1-78952-058-3
Gong – Kevan Furbank 978-1-78952-082-8
Green Day – William E. Spevack 978-1-78952-261-7
Hall And Oates – Ian Abrahams 978-1-78952-167-2
Hawkwind – Duncan Harris 978-1-78952-052-1
Peter Hammill – Richard Rees Jones 978-1-78952-163-4
Roy Harper – Opher Goodwin 978-1-78952-130-6
Jimi Hendrix – Emma Stott 978-1-78952-175-7
The Hollies – Andrew Darlington 978-1-78952-159-7
Horslips – Richard James 978-1-78952-263-1
The Human League And The Sheffield Scene –
Andrew Darlington 978-1-78952-186-3
The Incredible String Band – Tim Moon 978-1-78952-107-8
Iron Maiden – Steve Pilkington 978-1-78952-061-3
Joe Jackson – Richard James 978-1-78952-189-4
Jefferson Airplane – Richard Butterworth 978-1-78952-143-6
Jethro Tull – Jordan Blum 978-1-78952-016-3
Elton John In The 1970s – Peter Kearns 978-1-78952-034-7
Billy Joel – Lisa Torem 978-1-78952-183-2

Also available from Sonicbond

Judas Priest – John Tucker 978-1-78952-018-7
Kansas – Kevin Cummings 978-1-78952-057-6
The Kinks – Martin Hutchinson 978-1-78952-172-6
Korn – Matt Karpe 978-1-78952-153-5
Led Zeppelin – Steve Pilkington 978-1-78952-151-1
Level 42 – Matt Philips 978-1-78952-102-3
Little Feat – Georg Purvis - 978-1-78952-168-9
Aimee Mann – Jez Rowden 978-1-78952-036-1
Joni Mitchell – Peter Kearns 978-1-78952-081-1
The Moody Blues – Geoffrey Feakes 978-1-78952-042-2
Motorhead – Duncan Harris 978-1-78952-173-3
Nektar – Scott Meze – 978-1-78952-257-0
New Order – Dennis Remmer – 978-1-78952-249-5
Nightwish – Simon Mcmurdo – 978-1-78952-270-9
Laura Nyro – Philip Ward 978-1-78952-182-5
Mike Oldfield – Ryan Yard 978-1-78952-060-6
Opeth – Jordan Blum 978-1-78-952-166-5
Pearl Jam – Ben L. Connor 978-1-78952-188-7
Tom Petty – Richard James 978-1-78952-128-3
Pink Floyd – Richard Butterworth 978-1-78952-242-6
The Police – Pete Braidis 978-1-78952-158-0
Porcupine Tree – Nick Holmes 978-1-78952-144-3
Queen – Andrew Wild 978-1-78952-003-3
Radiohead – William Allen 978-1-78952-149-8
Rancid – Paul Matts 989-1-78952-187-0
Renaissance – David Detmer 978-1-78952-062-0
Reo Speedwagon – Jim Romag 978-1-78952-262-4
The Rolling Stones 1963-80 – Steve Pilkington 978-1-78952-017-0
The Smiths And Morrissey – Tommy Gunnarsson 978-1-78952-140-5
Spirit – Rev. Keith A. Gordon – 978-1-78952- 248-8
Stackridge – Alan Draper 978-1-78952-232-7
Status Quo The Frantic Four Years – Richard James 978-1-78952-160-3
Steely Dan – Jez Rowden 978-1-78952-043-9
Steve Hackett – Geoffrey Feakes 978-1-78952-098-9
Tears For Fears – Paul Clark - 978-178952-238-9
Thin Lizzy – Graeme Stroud 978-1-78952-064-4
Tool – Matt Karpe 978-1-78952-234-1
Toto – Jacob Holm-Lupo 978-1-78952-019-4
U2 – Eoghan Lyng 978-1-78952-078-1
Ufo – Richard James 978-1-78952-073-6
Van Der Graaf Generator – Dan Coffey 978-1-78952-031-6
Van Halen – Morgan Brown – 9781-78952-256-3
The Who – Geoffrey Feakes 978-1-78952-076-7
Roy Wood And The Move – James R Turner 978-1-78952-008-8
Yes – Stephen Lambe 978-1-78952-001-9
Frank Zappa 1966 To 1979 – Eric Benac 978-1-78952-033-0
Warren Zevon – Peter Gallagher 978-1-78952-170-2
10cc – Peter Kearns 978-1-78952-054-5

Decades Series

The Bee Gees In The 1960s – Andrew Mon Hughes Et Al 978-1-78952-148-1
The Bee Gees In The 1970s – Andrew Mon Hughes Et Al 978-1-78952-179-5
Black Sabbath In The 1970s – Chris Sutton 978-1-78952-171-9
Britpop – Peter Richard Adams And Matt Pooler 978-1-78952-169-6
Phil Collins In The 1980s – Andrew Wild 978-1-78952-185-6
Alice Cooper In The 1970s – Chris Sutton 978-1-78952-104-7

Alice Cooper In The 1980s – Chris Sutton 978-1-78952-259-4
Curved Air In The 1970s – Laura Shenton 978-1-78952-069-9
Donovan In The 1960s – Jeff Fitzgerald 978-1-78952-233-4
Bob Dylan In The 1980s – Don Klees 978-1-78952-157-3
Brian Eno In The 1970s – Gary Parsons 978-1-78952-239-6
Faith No More In The 1990s – Matt Karpe 978-1-78952-250-1
Fleetwood Mac In The 1970s – Andrew Wild 978-1-78952-105-4
Fleetwood Mac In The 1980s – Don Klees 978-178952-254-9
Focus In The 1970s – Stephen Lambe 978-1-78952-079-8
Free And Bad Company In The 1970s – John Van Der Kiste 978-1-78952-178-8
Genesis In The 1970s – Bill Thomas 978178952-146-7
George Harrison In The 1970s – Eoghan Lyng 978-1-78952-174-0
Kiss In The 1970s – Peter Gallagher 978-1-78952-246-4
Manfred Mann's Earth Band In The 1970s – John Van Der Kiste 978178952-243-3
Marillion In The 1980s – Nathaniel Webb 978-1-78952-065-1
Van Morrison In The 1970s – Peter Childs - 978-1-78952-241-9
Mott The Hoople And Ian Hunter In The 1970s –
John Van Der Kiste 978-1-78-952-162-7
Pink Floyd In The 1970s – Georg Purvis 978-1-78952-072-9
Suzi Quatro In The 1970s – Darren Johnson 978-1-78952-236-5
Queen In The 1970s – James Griffiths 978-1-78952-265-5
Roxy Music In The 1970s – Dave Thompson 978-1-78952-180-1
Slade In The 1970s – Darren Johnson 978-1-78952-268-6
Status Quo In The 1980s – Greg Harper 978-1-78952-244-0
Tangerine Dream In The 1970s – Stephen Palmer 978-1-78952-161-0
The Sweet In The 1970s – Darren Johnson 978-1-78952-139-9
Uriah Heep In The 1970s – Steve Pilkington 978-1-78952-103-0
Van Der Graaf Generator In The 1970s – Steve Pilkington 978-1-78952-245-7
Rick Wakeman In The 1970s – Geoffrey Feakes 978-1-78952-264-8
Yes In The 1980s – Stephen Lambe With David Watkinson 978-1-78952-125-2

On Screen Series
Carry On... – Stephen Lambe 978-1-78952-004-0
David Cronenberg – Patrick Chapman 978-1-78952-071-2
James Bond – Andrew Wild 978-1-78952-010-1
Monty Python – Steve Pilkington 978-1-78952-047-7

Other Books
1967: A Year In Psychedelic Rock 978-1-78952-155-9
1970: A Year In Rock – John Van Der Kiste 978-1-78952-147-4
1973: The Golden Year Of Progressive Rock 978-1-78952-165-8
Babysitting A Band On The Rocks – G.d. Praetorius 978-1-78952-106-1
Eric Clapton Sessions – Andrew Wild 978-1-78952-177-1
Derek Taylor: For Your Radioactive Children –
Andrew Darlington 978-1-78952-038-5
The Golden Road: The Recording History Of The Grateful Dead – John Kilbride 978-1-78952-156-6
Iggy And The Stooges On Stage 1967-1974 – Per Nilsen 978-1-78952-101-6
Jon Anderson And The Warriors – The Road To Yes –
David Watkinson 978-1-78952-059-0
Magic: The David Paton Story – David Paton 978-1-78952-266-2
Misty: The Music Of Johnny Mathis – Jakob Baekgaard 978-1-78952-247-1
Nu Metal: A Definitive Guide – Matt Karpe 978-1-78952-063-7
Tommy Bolin: In And Out Of Deep Purple – Laura Shenton 978-1-78952-070-5
Maximum Darkness – Deke Leonard 978-1-78952-048-4
The Twang Dynasty – Deke Leonard 978-1-78952-049-1

And Many More To Come!